**Amgueddfa Genedlaethol Cymru
National Museum of Wales
Cardiff 1986**

Cardiff Shipowners

by J. Geraint Jenkins and David Jenkins

Acknowledgements

To list the many persons who have contributed in some way to the writing of this booklet would require an amount of space quite disproportionate to its text. Suffice to say, therefore, that we are most grateful to those people, many of whom were, or are, in some way connected with shipowning at Cardiff, without whose assistance this book could not have been envisaged. In this way no-one is left out, and everyone is acknowledged!

Most of the illustrations in the book are from the museum's photographic archive; those illustrations acquired from other sources are individually acknowledged.

J. Geraint Jenkins, Curator
David Jenkins, Research Assistant

Welsh Industrial and Maritime Museum,
Cardiff

Introduction

Cardiff was the boom town of late Victorian Britain. For a few years before 1914, the port outstripped both London and Liverpool for the amount of cargo handled at its docks and fortunes were made by the many shipowners of Cardiff who owned a vast fleet of tramp steamers. 'There is no more interesting study in town growth than Cardiff', said a Board of Trade Report of 1908. 'At the census of 1851 it was a place of some 20,000 inhabitants with no influence and no reputation, now it is one of the most thriving cities in the country, a centre of trade and commerce and a great port. In every respect the development has been remarkable.' The rise of Cardiff as a great commercial centre was almost unique in Britain and when contemporary writers sought parallels their only choice was Chicago.

The remarkable and sudden development had one driving force: the building of the Bute Docks and the amassing of an ever-increasing fortune by the Bute family. Cardiff, which stood astride the estuaries of three rivers was the natural gateway to the wealth of the Glamorgan valleys. During the second half of the nineteenth century a new assertive class of businessmen — merchants, coal factors and shipowners — rapidly took over the leadership of the community. These influential men, many of whom came from other parts of the country, built their own Merchants' Exchange at Pier Head while between 1883 and 1886 the coal owners and exporters built the spectacular Coal Exchange in the centre of the residential Mount Stuart Square. That building was renovated and made even more splendid in 1912 and it was the centre of probably the largest coal operation in the world. The power and influence of its members contributed in no small measure to the wealth of Cardiff and its hinterland.

Cardiff's prosperity was almost entirely based on the export of coal and of the record 13.7 million tons of cargoes exported from the port of Cardiff in 1913, no fewer than 10.5 million tons were in coal exports alone. Iron ore and pit props were imported in great quantities and Cardiff as a port was entirely dependent on heavy extractive and manufacturing industry. The dynamic influence of coal in particular is reflected in the spectacular growth of tramp shipowning in the port. Coal, iron ore and pit props were the very commodities in which the steam tramp steamer could gain superiority over the old sailing vessels. As port facilities in Cardiff were improved between 1859 with the opening of the Bute East Dock and the opening of the Queen Alexandra Dock in 1907, and as the railway links to the port's hinterland were developed, so too did the fleet of Cardiff tramp steamers multiply.

Until the eighteen fifties, Cardiff was of no great consequence as a shipowning port and most of the products of the South Wales valleys were exported through Cardiff in sailing vessels that belonged to other ports. It did have a few shipowners who operated small sailing vessels to the other ports of the Bristol Channel, but as a port, Cardiff had fewer shipowners than such rural ports as Cardigan and Aberystwyth. In 1850, for example, Cardiff possessed no more than 68 sailing vessels of an average capacity of 96 tons; by 1860 that figure had increased to a total of only 93 vessels with an average capacity of 150 tons. By the 1870s, however, the age of the tramp steamer had arrived, and steam gradually replaced sail on the world's oceans.

In 1857, William Cory, an immigrant to Cardiff from Hartland in Devon in association with the well-known coal-owner John Nixon purchased a new 1168 gross ton screw steamer, the *William Cory* from a Tyneside shipbuilder. The vessel, though London registered, was specifically used for the Cardiff coal trade and she was the first of a vast fleet of tramp steamers that were to play such a vital part in the economic life of South Wales for the next sixty years and more.

In 1865 the first Cardiff registered, Cardiff owned ship, the screw steamer *Llandaff* (411 gross tons) was purchased by the Cardiff docksman H. Vellacott from Schlesinger, the Tyneside shipbuilder. Within a year Vellacott purchased a second ship the *Fairwater* from Schlesinger. Another docksman Charles E. Stallybrass who already had shares in Velacott's enterprise, entered shipowning on his own account purchasing the *Leckwith* in 1868. Charles Stallybrass like so many of the other Cardiff shipowners was an immigrant, for he was born in Siberia in 1838, the son of a missionary whose claim to fame was that he translated the Bible into Mongolian. He came to Cardiff in 1857 and by 1876 he was an important figure in Cardiff's expanding docks owning five tramp steamers, engaged almost entirely in the coal trade.

The floodgates were open and the Cardiff tramp steamer fleet expanded at an enormous rate as more and more businessmen from all parts of Europe came to Cardiff and invested in ships. Undoubtedly Cardiff was the honeypot of Britain not only for aspiring shipowners but also for sailors, dockworkers, ship chandlers and hordes of others who came to the port to participate in its ever-increasing activity. From the Channel Islands came the Morel Brothers, J.B. Hacquoil and H.B. Marquand to establish what became highly successful shipping enterprises. Many newcomers came from the West of England, from Appledore, Padstow and Portland among them John Cory and his distant cousins the Cory Brothers, John and Richard, Edward Nicholl, John Angel Gibbs, W.J. Tatem and William Reardon Smith. Rural Wales and the long

An aerial view of Cardiff and its docks taken in 1950

The creator of modern Cardiff: John, 2nd Marquis of Bute, 1793-1848

tradition of seafaring from the remote creeks of Dyfed and Gwynedd supplied many shipowners who saw the opportunity for trade in the most dynamic and vibrant of all British ports. From the Ceredigion village of Aber-porth came Evan Thomas, the Jenkins Brothers and Thomas Owen of the Glanhowny Shipping Company, while from nearby Llangrannog came Evan Owen, *Y Foel* who established a shipowning enterprise in Cardiff. John Mathias, a substantial Aberystwyth shipowner also moved his centre of operations to Cardiff, as did the brothers Owen and Watkin Williams from the tiny village of Edern in the Llŷn Peninsula. Businessmen from the North East of England such as the

Turnbull Brothers, and Pyman Watson and Company, already well established in the north-east, also established offices in Cardiff while men from the European Continent, Sven Hansen from Norway, the Count de Lucovich from Trieste, M.L. Demetrios and Charles Cravos from Greece and the Guérét family from France also made Cardiff their headquarters.

Many of these immigrant shipowners still maintained their connections with their region of origin. For example, the Turnbull Bros. of Whitby in Yorkshire were largely financed from the north-east even after they had moved to

The Coal & Shipping Exchange, Cardiff as re-built in 1912

South Wales coal was to the world economy in the early twentieth century what oil is today

Cardiff. Much of Evan Thomas Radcliffe and Company's early capital was raised in rural West and North Wales and throughout their hundred year history, the majority of masters and officers that they employed were from the remote rural areas of Wales.

Becoming a shipowner was not all that difficult and a person of enterprise with little capital could easily raise enough money to finance a company. Although most of the early Cardiff tramp steamers were financed under the age-old 64th system whereby the shares in a vessel were divided into 64 shares, as time progressed it became necessary to introduce a new type of financial structure. The limited liability, joint stock company, and especially the single ship company became the means to ensure the capitalisation of an ever-expanding fleet. Thus for every vessel there could be hundreds of shareholders, some of them investing only a few pounds in a ship. In the good years, dividends were high, but in the bad years, ruin could face the small investor who had staked his life savings in a Cardiff shipping company. The person who really profited from operating a single-ship company was the manager, the person who had floated the company. Very often he had little financial stake in a company, but he took a commission on gross earnings rather than on profits, so that provided he was getting a freight he was not greatly concerned with the profitability of the company's operation. The system did have advantages in that a great deal of capital could be raised very quickly, much of it through the action of share pushers and widespread publicity. High dividends obtained by well-established firms were always well publicised and many people were persuaded to invest in new single ship companies, some of which were established by entrepreneurs described as 'rash and unscrupulous speculators'.

A number of aspiring Cardiff shipowners did actually abscond after collecting money subscribed by investors before delivery of a ship. Managers of single ship companies, says Robin Craig, 'could secure for themselves virtual insulation from the risks inherent in traditional forms of shipowning. By making management and other fees a prior call on the revenue of companies regardless of whether or not the ships were making a profit, unscrupulous promoters maximised income and left the risk to be borne by the unfortunate investors. Often there were concealed payments to the managers of which the investors were entirely unaware.' Some Cardiff shipowners certainly earned for themselves a dubious reputation and a number of insurance underwriters demanded additional premiums to cover Cardiff-owned ships during the early years of the present century. 'Marine casualties' were not unknown and over-insurance was rife, with the result that a number of Cardiff shipowners opened London branches and had their vessels registered in that port in an attempt to escape the odium of owning Cardiff-registered vessels. Despite the bad

Coal awaiting transhipment in the Roath dock marshalling sidings

'The men who made the world go round'; members of the Cardiff and Bristol Channel Incorporated Shipowners Association, 1916

reputation enjoyed by the more unscrupulous of owners, the majority were above reproach and were highly successful, providing excellent returns for thousands of investors.

Between the 1860s and 1914 Cardiff was one of the principal tramp ship owning ports in Europe. In 1913 tramp shipping accounted for 60% of British tonnage and at that time, coal employed about 40% or about 3 million tons of British tramps. The coal carrying capacity of Cardiff registered ships in 1907 was 1.3 million deadweight tons. This was the time of opportunity as more and more men entered shipowning with the result that by 1910, 367 ships that sailed the world's oceans were Cardiff owned. Small businessmen became millionaires as the result of worldwide demand for Welsh coal to drive factories, steamships and railway engines. W.J. Tatem, for example, a native of Appledore, Devon after working as a clerk in a Cardiff shipping office started his own business in 1897 and was soon running as many as fifteen single ship companies. By 1906 he could claim to be the largest individual shipowner in Cardiff having built up a fleet of 150,000 tons deadweight in a matter of seven years.

The end of the First World War witnessed a remarkable boom in the history of shipowning in Cardiff. Many ships had been lost during the war, there was dislocation at the ports and this led to a huge rise in freight rates. New men entered the industry; small-time owners became owners of substantial fleets, and 'ship owning at Cardiff developed from a business to a craze. The port became the centre of a great shipping boom which attracted millions of pounds from investors and speculators in all parts of the United Kingdom.' Among these newer owners were some, like Samuel Instone, Sven Hansen and the Harrisons of the Town Line, who expanded their interests with the purchase of collieries in addition to their shipping interests. In this way they built up concerns that handled every aspect of the coal trade from the hewing of the coal to its export abroad, handled by their own agents in dozens of foreign importing ports.

By the end of 1920, Cardiff could boast 122 shipping companies that owned some 1.5 million gross tons of shipping, which raised it to the status of the greatest steamship-owning centre in the world. The boom was also characterised by the disappearance of many of Cardiff's older shipping firms, forced out of business by war-time losses and the effects of the Excess Profits Duty, imposed during the war, and not relaxed until 1926. These old-established firms were replaced by new companies under the management of ambitious yet un-tried men who were largely unaware of the violent fluctuations that could affect the tramp-shipping market. Such a violent

A crowded Queen Alexandra Dock in 1920

By the late 1950s, Cardiff's docks were a mere shadow of their former selves

fluctuation occurred late in 1920, as freight rates tumbled to less than a quarter of those prevailing twelve months previously. This dramatic collapse could be attributed to a number of factors — the advent of oil as a maritime fuel, the revival of continental collieries after the ravages of the war and the flooding of the European market with German reparation coal — and its effects on Cardiff were catastrophic. The local newspapers of the early 1920s were full of reports of the bankruptcy of many of Cardiff's newer shipowners, who found themselves facing ruin as they were forced to sell off their vessels for a sixth of the price that they had paid for them during the boom.

It was a blow from which Cardiff, both as a port and a shipowning centre, never recovered. Throughout the twenties and thirties, until the eve of the Second World War, freight rates remained low; many companies folded and those that survived were forced to participate in the world-wide tramping trades to survive. Even then many companies found themselves unable to declare dividends and were forced to lay-up their vessels for extended periods. Many Cardiff owners were, moreover, slow to adopt motor vessels as opposed to the steamers on which the port's prosperity had been founded; in the late thirties prominent Cardiff firms were still building steam-propelled vessels whose basic design had remained largely unchanged for half a century. By 1937, there were but 57 companies left at Cardiff, controlling 545,000 gross tons of shipping. The post-war era has seen a continuation in that decline. Coal exports from Cardiff ceased in 1964 and by today there are only two Cardiff-based firms that actually own ships. Today the Bute Docks at Cardiff are a mere shadow of their former glory and the Bute Street — Mount Stuart Square area of the city is no longer the centre of some of the most extensive tramp-owning enterprises in the world. Many of the resplendent office buildings from which the coal trade of the world was once controlled are now empty or demolished and the days when Cardiff's Butetown was one of the world's most vital and industrious shipping centres have long since gone.

Some Pioneers

The first Cardiff-registered, Cardiff-owned steamship was the Llandaff, completed on the Tyne in 1865 and owned by a consortium headed by H.J. Vellacott. She continued to trade under various different owners until she was stranded off Land's End in October 1899 and declared a total constructive loss

A shareholder in the Llandaff, who later became a prominent early shipowner in his own right, was Charles Ellah Stallybrass. He died in 1922 at the age of 84, and regularly attended the Exchange right up until his death

Francis Hacquoil, like the Morels, was a native of the Channel Islands. By 1876, his company owned three iron steamers

John Gower Marychurch was one of the few early pioneers of steamship owning at Cardiff who was actually born in the port. His father had owned a number of wooden sailing vessels at Cardiff, but upon his death in 1870, John Marychurch moved into steamships, and by 1880 he was operating four iron steamers

*The Exmouth was built in 1899 for Messrs. J.H. Anning of Cardiff.
The Annings were natives of Appledore, and were among the first
Westcountrymen to set up in business as shipowners at Cardiff. Initially
they operated only sailing vessels, but from 1877 onwards, they began to invest in
steamships. Though never a large company, Annings were of considerable
significance in the history of shipowning at Cardiff as both Henry Radcliffe and
W.J. Tatem began their careers in the Anning offices while William Reardon
Smith served as a master with the firm in the 1890s*

Morel Ltd.

The brothers Philip and Thomas Morel moved to Cardiff from their native
Jersey in 1857 and 1862 respectively, having previously been involved in the
important potato trade from the Channel Islands to South Wales. Initially
concerned with the chartering and ownership of sailing vessels in the Spanish
ore and South American coal trades, they acquired their first steamship, the
Colstrup in 1876. By 1888, they owned twenty-three tramp steamers; they had
built up what amounted to a near monopoly of the iron trade from Bilbao to
South Wales, and this trade was complemented by outward exports of Welsh
coal to French ports such as Brest or Nantes.

The Morels were among the few Cardiff shipowners to encourage shipbuilding
at Cardiff, when in 1882 they acquired what later came to be known as the
Bute Shipbuilding, Engineering and Dry Dock Co. on the banks of the River
Taf. Apart from repair work, three new ships were built at this yard between
1886 and 1890, but the lack of adequate local engineering facilities and disputes
with the Bute estate over leases hampered developments to such a degree that
no further ships were built at Cardiff.

The founding partners, Philip and Thomas, died in 1908 and 1903 respectively,
but by the eve of the First World War, the firm was operating a fleet of eleven
vessels engaged chiefly by this date upon the 'coal out, grain home' trade to
South America. After the war, disagreements between the descendants of the
two founders had led to the sale of the remaining vessels, and it was not until
1921 that Thomas Morel's sons, Thomas and Ralph, began to rebuild the fleet.
By 1935 the firm operated four vessels, and from 1936 onwards, they built a
number of new motor vessels during a period when many Cardiff owners still
clung doggedly to steam propulsion.

Four vessels were lost during the Second World War, and with the decline of
the coal trade from South Wales during the post-war years the firm moved its
centre of operations to London, concentrating on world-wide tramping. With
these developments in mind, three new motor vessels were ordered in 1951.
Delivered in 1953-54, these ships had a very short life under Morel ownership
as it was decided, in view of the increasingly gloomy outlook for small
tramping firms, to dispose of the remaining vessels in 1956. Liquidation started
in 1957 and the entire capital of the firm was dispersed to the shareholders
by 1960.

Sir Thomas Morel

Philip Morel

A view of the Bute Shipbuilding, Engineering and Dry Dock Co.'s yard on the River Taf in 1884

St. Andrew's House, Thomas Morel's home at Dinas Powys, completed in 1892

The Pontypridd, completed in 1924 by the Northumberland Shipbuilding Co., Newcastle-upon-Tyne

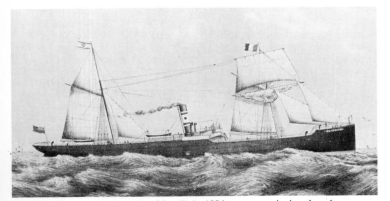

The Blaenavon, completed for Morel's in 1881, was a typical early schooner-rigged tramp steamer

The Jersey Dawn was one of three handsome motor tramps built for Morel's in 1953-4

John Cory & Sons Ltd.

John Cory was one of the earliest owners of steamships in Cardiff, for the highly successful venture he established in the port goes back to 1872 when an already successful West Country shipowner and his family arrived in Cardiff from Padstow. John Cory was born in Padstow in 1823, the son of a farmer. He went to sea, but in 1854 he established his own business by purchasing the coastal ketch *Millicent* that had been built on the banks of the River Camel in 1844. In 1862, with the sale of the *Millicent,* the brigantine *Volunteer,* built on Prince Edward Island in Canada was purchased and in the same year the large barque *John Henry* a Newport-built, Newport-owned vessel joined the fleet. The *Volunteer* was Cardiff-registered and this marked the first real contact between a Padstow shipowner and a South Wales port. In 1863, John Cory retired from the sea in order to manage his sailing vessels from an office in Padstow; one of the main cargoes carried in the early days being the lucrative contract to transport Cornish granite from Padstow to London to build the Thames Embankment. Nevertheless, in the 1860s with the silting of the estuary of the Camel, and declining cargoes, Padstow was becoming a maritime backwater and in 1872 the Cory family moved to Cardiff that was rapidly growing into a great port.

The rise of the company was very rapid. 'With two ships operating and two new ones of vastly improved dimensions on order, a growing shipbroking business and a newly started interest in iron ore importing from Bilbao, an office was set up in Cardiff Docks.' With his sons John (1855-1930) and Herbert (1857-1933) (later Sir Herbert Cory, Bart.), John Cory was in the front rank of shipowners. In 1876 the fleet had grown to 10 vessels; in 1898 it had increased to 23 and business as iron ore merchants, timber importers and coal exporters had grown phenomenally. In that year, too, the company built its present offices on the corner of Mount Stuart Square and James Street, premises that it still occupies.

Many of the vessels built on the north-east coast of England for John Cory & Co during the first decade of the 20th century were shallow draught vessels designed for the Spanish ore trade and the many shallow ports of northern Spain. The company had an interest in dry docks and shipbuilding on the Tees and even owned an hotel at Padstow. At the outbreak of war in 1914, John Cory & Sons was among the most successful of Cardiff businesses with 23 ships and a world-wide market for its unique blend of coal, 'Cory's Pacific Navigation Large Steam Coal'. Unfortunately, during the war, 20 Cory vessels were sunk and at the end of the war Cory's emerged with nine ships, fewer

John Cory's first vessel was the coasting ketch, Millicent, *bought in 1854*

than half the pre-war fleet, in spite of several replacements. It was not until 1925 that three new vessels the SS's *Ruperra, Ramillies* and *Coryton* were delivered. By 1936 with the decline of the coal exporting business, Cory possessed only three ships which were all to be lost during the Second World War. In 1946 it had two vessels — *Ramillies* (built 1942) and *Ravenshoe* (built 1945) but by 1955 only one vessel — a new *Ramillies* built in 1951 was owned by the company. Although the Cardigan S.S.Co. with its single ship was purchased in 1957, the company ceased to be shipowners in 1966. John Cory & Sons Ltd. are still in business today as shipbrokers and travel agents and still occupy the splendid buildings designed by Sir Herbert Cory's son-in-law, Tudor Thornley in 1898.

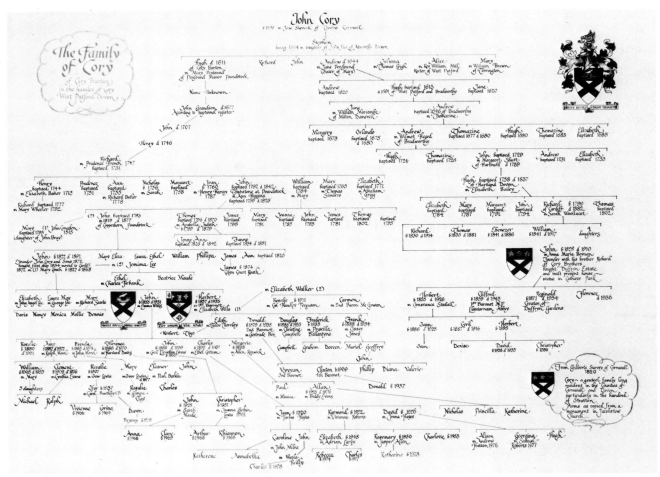

The pedigree of the Cory families in Devon and Cornwall

John Cory, eldest son of the founder of John Cory & Sons

The Cory's offices on the corner of James St. and Mountstuart Square in Butetown

The Restormel *approaching Cardiff docks in 1965*

The Ramillies *discharging pitwood at Cardiff in 1937*

Evan Jones & Co. — the Field Line (Cardiff) Ltd.

The former county of Caernarfonshire was well-known for its maritime associations and during the latter half of the nineteenth century produced a number of eminent Liverpool-Welsh shipowners who moved to that port from their native area to take full advantage of the commercial opportunities that Merseyside offered. Not all of them moved to Liverpool, however; in 1865, Evan Jones left his native Porthmadog and established himself at Cardiff, where by 1880 he was the owner of three substantial wooden barques operating in the South American coal trade.

Relatively few Cardiff shipowners successfully completed the transition from sail to steam, but in 1883 Evan Jones purchased a new iron tramp steamer of 1,382 gross tons, the *South Wales,* followed a year later by the *South Cambria* of 2,000 gross tons. Evan Jones died in 1891 and was succeeded by his son, W. Watkin Jones, who by 1896 had disposed of the firm's last sailing vessel and was operating a fleet of three tramp steamers. Apart from his shipping interests, W.W. Jones was also a director of numerous ship-repairing and colliery companies and in 1896 was chairman of the Cardiff Shipowners' Association.

By the end of 1900, due to losses and sales, the firm was left with no vessel whatsoever, but in 1902 the bankruptcy of John Ruthen, another Cardiff shipowner, provided Watkin Jones with the opportunity to acquire five relatively modern steamers. Ruthen's vessels were all named with the *'-field'* suffix, and thus it was that Watkin Jones decided to form one new joint-stock venture (in place of the three single-ship companies operated before 1900) bearing the title The Field Line (Cardiff) Ltd. This particular form of title was adopted to avoid confusion with the Field Steamship Co. of Stockton-on-Tees.

This fleet was maintained with no changes during the first decade of the present century and the five vessels participated in the traditional Cardiff tramping trades to the Mediterranean and Black Seas, and to the River Plate. With the advent of the First World War and the effects of the Excess Profits Duty (introduced in 1915 and increased in 1917) Watkin Jones decided to dispose of three of his steamers in 1917. The two remaining vessels, *Eastfield* and *Westfield* remained in service with the Field Line until 1919, when advantage was taken of the high prices being fetched by tonnage during the post-war boom to sell both steamers. The company remained in existence until at least 1923; with the slump that followed during the 1920s, however, Watkin Jones was understandably not keen to re-enter into shipowning and thus the link between Porthmadog and Cardiff, arguably Wales's two most fascinating mineral exporting ports, was brought to an end.

Evan Jones was a native of Porthmadog, one of Gwynedd's great slate exporting ports

W. Watkin Jones succeeded his father as managing owner of the enterprise in 1891

The Northfield, *built in 1901, as portrayed by a Neapolitan pierhead artist*

The Westfield *was the Field Line's last vessel when she was sold in 1919.*
(World Ship Photo Library)

A.T. de Lucovich

Of all the colourful characters that operated in Cardiff dockland at the height of its prosperity, undoubtedly the most interesting was Antonio Leonardo Trifone, the Count de Lucovich. He was an impressive figure with a full beard whose noble ancestry on the Adriatic coast could be traced back for many centuries. He was a Knight of the Order of Francis Joseph I and Admiral of the Noble Corps of Bocchesi Mariners. Antonio de Lucovich was born in Cattario, Dalmazia, then part of the Austro-Hungarian Empire in 1832. In 1848, he began his studies for a law qualification at the University of Parma, and despite severe opposition from his noble family, he entered the world of commerce rather than law. In 1850 he arrived in Cardiff, then growing to a position of importance as a coal exporting port. Within a few years A.T. de Lucovich had set up a flourishing coal exporting and shipbroking business mainly for the export of coal from Cardiff to Italy and the Adriatic ports. Obviously his own area of origin was the principal area of interest and when in the 1870s he decided to go into shipowning, the vessels he owned were all registered at Trieste and all carried Italian names. They were sailing ships — the *Cavalier Krapf* (346 tons, built Sunderland 1869 and owned by de Lucovich from 1881 to 1887); the *Conte Iginio L* (463 tons, built Sunderland 1864, owned by the company from 1886 to 1893); the *Conte Arturo L* (518 tons, built Istria 1872, owned 1890-2); *Conte Oscar L* (957 tons, built Spotorno 1871, owned 1890-3); *Isabella* (346 tons, built Littlehampton 1871, owned 1896-9). The Count de Lucovich did not remain in shipowning for long and by 1899 he had sold his last vessel. Nevertheless, as a broker and head of a coal exporting company of de Lucovich, Banaz and Harte he had a very successful career in Cardiff docks. The company was very closely associated with shipowning companies in Trieste, Venice, Fiume and Split and as far south as the Adriatic ports of Dubrovnik and Kotor. Banaz (Banac) was equally distinguished for he was associated with the renowned Racic family of shipowners of Dubrovnik and he himself was the Serbian representative at the Versailles peace conference. Banaz in the post world war period became a very flourishing Jugoslav shipowner, owning a substantial fleet of cargo and passenger vessels. His yacht *Nahlua* was used by the Duke of Windsor and his intended wife, Mrs. Wallis Simpson, on an Adriatic cruise in the 1930s.

Antonio de Lucovich who died in 1913 had many business interests in Cardiff. He was Chairman of Hills Dry Dock Company with its graving docks in both the East and West Docks. He was also Chairman of the R.W. Patent Fuel Company at Newport and Cardiff. The production of patent fuel was of considerable importance in South Wales. Small coal was bonded with pitch under heat and the resulting fuel was easily transported to all parts of the world in blocks, complete with the impressed trade mark of the manufacturing company. The fuel blocks stacked well and did not lose their volatility.

Antonio Leonardo Trifone, the Count de Lucovich

Evan Thomas, Radcliffe & Co. Ltd.

In 1983 one of the principal Cardiff shipowners that had been in existence for just over a hundred years ceased to own any ships. Evan Thomas was a master mariner, a native of the Ceredigion coastal village of Aber-porth. That village had a long history of maritime activity for not only was it the great centre of the Cardigan Bay herring industry but it also saw great commercial activity. Until the arrival of the railway at Newcastle Emlyn and Cardigan in the late nineteenth century, the essentials of life were brought in by sea. Hezekiah Thomas (1805-69) was very much concerned with the maritime coastal trade, but his son Evan (1832-1891) sailed not from his native village but from the great port of Cardiff. He obtained his master's certificate and after eight years sailing deep sea he set up a shipping company in association with a Merthyr Tudful shipping clerk, Henry Radcliffe (1857-1921). Although they had little money themselves they were able, without much difficulty, to raise capital and had a steamer — the *Gwenllian Thomas,* built by Palmers of Jarrow-on-Tyne for £17,750. The business succeeded beyond their wildest dreams and within the next three years they purchased four more brand new vessels. Evan Thomas gave up seafaring in 1884 to concentrate on the business and by the time he died in 1891 the company that had been established less than ten years previously controlled as many as 15 new tramp steamers.

Undoubtedly, the success of the Aber-porth seaman and the Merthyr Tudful businessman was partly due to the ease with which they were able to raise capital; a great deal of it from rural Wales. Evan Thomas's brother-in-law Jenkin David was a bank manager in Dolgellau and he was able to direct many of his customers — railwaymen and quarry workers, Nonconformist ministers and woollen manufacturers — to invest their savings in the Cardiff shipping company with which he was closely associated. The most notable of Evan Thomas's advocates, however, was a pillar of the Nonconformist pulpit — the Rev. J. Cynddylan Jones — a Cardi. Since Evan Thomas paid him 2% of all the profits derived by his companies in the 1880s, Cynddylan was more than ready to persuade members of congregations throughout Wales to invest in the shipping company. 'He deserves to be appointed Chaplain to the fleet', said one newspaper report, 'provided that the fleet requires a chaplain'. The Rev. Jones gradually became disillusioned and dissatisfied with his remuneration for share pushing and he demanded four shares in all the company's ships. That request was refused and with Evan Thomas's early death in 1891, Cynddylan was never again associated with the firm of Evan Thomas Radcliffe & Co. The company, run by Henry Radcliffe and his brother Daniel (1860-1933) went from strength to strength and by 1900 they controlled as many as 24 steamships.

A shipping company such as Radcliffe with its roots deep in rural Wales drew very heavily on the coastal villages of Cardigan Bay for men to man their vessels. As the coastal trade in Dyfed and Gwynedd declined in the late 19th century many of the mariners of those remote regions began sailing in Cardiff vessels, though many of them still retained their homes in their villages of origin. Thus in 1890 no fewer than 12 of the 15 steamers owned by Evan Thomas, Radcliffe & Co were captained by mariners from West Wales. That association was to continue for as long as the company existed.

Undoubtedly the business was a highly successful one. In 1914, for example, the company possessed 28 vessels of which no fewer than 20 were sunk during the war. With substantial compensation for war losses the company had the capital to invest in new vessels during the latter half of the 1920s. As many as eight new ships were built in 1928-9 with the result that in 1930, Radcliffe was among the most important of all Cardiff shipowners with a fleet of 16 vessels. Again the Second World War was disastrous with no fewer than 11 of their 15 vessels being sunk. Despite replacement only 5 ships were owned by the company in 1946, a figure that was to remain constant until 1970. By 1981, with all the ships disposed of, the company attempted to operate two small coasters, an attempt that failed with the sale of both vessels in 1983.

The Gwenllian Thomas, *completed at Jarrow in 1882*

Henry Radcliffe

Captain Evan Thomas

'Chaplain to the fleet': the Rev. John Cynddylan Jones. (National Library of Wales, Aberystwyth)

BILL OF SALE.

| Official Number of Ship *78442* | | Name of Ship *Gwenllian Thomas* |

| Port Number and Year of Registry. *4/1882* | Port of Registry *Swansea* | British or Foreign built. *British* | How propelled *Screw Steam* | Where built *Jarrow* | When built *1882* |

						Feet.	Tenths.
Number of Decks	*One and a break*	Build	*Clincher*	Length from forepart of Stem, under the bowsprit, to the aft side of the Head of the Stern-post		*225*	*4*
Number of Masts	*Two*	Galleries	*None*	Mainbreadth to outside of Plank		*31*	*2*
Rigged	*Schooner*	Head	*None*	Depth in Hold from Tonnage Deck to Ceiling at Midships		*17*	
Stern	*Elliptic*	Framework	*Iron*	Depth in Hold from Upper Deck to Ceiling at Midships in the case of three Decks and upwards			
				Length of Engine Room, if any		*34*	*7*

	No. of Engines.	Description.	Whether British or Foreign made	When made	Name and Address of Makers.	Diameter of Cylinders	Length of Stroke	No. of Horses' Power combined.
Particulars of Engines, (if any)	*Two*	*Inverted direct acting Compound surface condensing*	*British*	*1882*	*Palmers Ship Building and Iron Company Limited Newcastle on Tyne*	*28 a 52 a*	*33 a*	*99*

GROSS TONNAGE.		No. of Tons.	DEDUCTIONS ALLOWED.		No. of Tons.
Under Tonnage Deck		*970·29*	On account of Space required for Propelling Power		*366·46*
Closed-in Spaces above Tonnage Deck, if any, Space or Spaces between Deck			On account of Spaces occupied by Seamen or Apprentices, appropriated to their use, and kept free from Goods and Stores of every kind not being the personal property of the Crew. These Spaces are the following, viz.:		
Poop Break		*60·98*	*Lower Forecastle Sailors*		
Bridge		*89·67*	Port		*22·11*
Roundhouse Side Houses		*5·60*	Second officer		*3·57*
Other closed-in Spaces, if any, as follows *Chart House*		*2·28*	*Second and Third Engineers, Fore officers*		*21·70*
Lines of Hatchways		*10·58*	*Mess Room, First Engineer*		
Gross Tonnage		*1446·13*			
Deductions as per Contra		*414·24*	Total Deductions		*414·24*
Registered Tonnage		*731·89*			

I Evan Thomas of Porthcawl in the county of Glamorgan Ship Owner in consideration of the sum of *Two hundred Eighty two pounds Seventeen shillings three pence* paid to *me* by *David Jones of Abercarn in the County of Glamorgan Licensed Victualler* the Receipt whereof is hereby acknowledged, transfer *One* Share in the Ship above particularly described, and in her boats, guns, ammunition, small arms, and appurtenances to the said *David Jones*

Further, the said *Evan Thomas* for *myself / my* heirs, covenant with the said *David Jones* and *his* assigns, that *I* have power to transfer in manner aforesaid the premises herein-before expressed to be transferred, and that the same are free from incumbrances

In witness whereof *I* ha *ve* hereunto subscribed *my* name and affixed *my* seal this *Ninth* day of *January* One thousand eight hundred and *Eighty three*

Executed by the above-named *Evan Thomas*
in the presence of *Henry Radcliffe 18 Bute Docks Cardiff*

Evan Thomas

"I" or "we."

†"Me" or "us."

‡"I" or "we."
§"Myself and my" or "ourselves and our."
‖"His," "her," or "their."
¶"I" or "we."
**If there be any subsisting Mortgage, or outstanding Certificate of Mortgage, add "save as appears by the Registry of the said Ship."

NOTE.—A Purchaser of a Registered British Vessel does not obtain a complete title until the Bill of Sale has been recorded at the Port of Registry of the Ship; and neglect of this precaution may entail serious consequences.

F & T 23/00 5-81 [19-3-36] 196.

No. 460.

A bill of sale of one sixty-fourth of the Gwenllian Thomas *to* David Jones, *a publican from Abercarn*

The Wimborne, *built in 1911, entering Antwerp in 1922*

Radcliffe's marine superintendent for many years was Captain B.T. Morris of Bryngwyn near Newcastle Emlyn. Here he is seen with his wife at the launch of the Llandilo *in 1928*

The Peterston *was one of a number of new steamers built for Radcliffe's in the 1920s*

The Llantrisant, *completed by Bartrams of Sunderland in 1958*

Charles Radcliffe & Co. Ltd.

The Radcliffe family were among the best-known of all Cardiff shipowners and the brothers Henry and Daniel ran one of the largest tramp steamer fleets in the port. They had a younger brother, Charles, less flamboyant and less ambitious than his brothers, but nevertheless a very successful docksman. Charles was born in Merthyr Tudful in 1862, the son of a stonemason who worked at the famous Penydarren Ironworks. He soon followed his brothers to Cardiff, but unlike them he did not enter any of the rapidly expanding business houses of dockland. Henry was already employed by the shipowner J.H. Anning before he embarked on his own business with Evan Thomas in 1881 and Daniel worked as an accounting clerk for another well-known Cardiff ship company, the Turnbulls of Whitby before joining his brother in 1891. Charles entered the Civil Service and for two years worked in the Marine Division of the Board of Trade at its Cardiff office.

Perhaps the call of commerce was too strong, or perhaps he could see the great success his older brother Henry was making of his business, but in 1891, with the death of Capt. Evan Thomas, he was for a short time associated with the Radcliffe company. That association was not to last long, for in 1891 Charles, in partnership with his brother Daniel, was managing the Glamorgan Steamship Company and its single vessel — the *Lady Armstrong*. That fraternal partnership was to last until 1913, the company being responsible for managing the 1892 Whitby-built 2,768 gross ton vessel, the *Peterston*. Charles was not even a director of the family firm of Evan Thomas, Radcliffe and Company, but in 1901 he entered shipowning on his own account, purchasing the *Craiglea*. Later in the first decade of this century he set up a number of single-ship companies — the Rochdale, Snowdon and Birkdale companies with a fleet of five vessels. In 1914, Charles Radcliffe owned the *Rochdale*, *Snowdon*, *Reresby*, *Atherstone* and *Penstone*.

In addition to his shipowning activities, Charles Radcliffe was the founder, managing director and secretary of the Tydfil Engineering and Ship Repairing Company located between the Roath Dock and East Bute Dock and this company, established around 1892, employed as many as 300 men. Charles, said to be a retiring man, was well known as a breeder of hackney horses.

The shipowning business was a successful one and despite losses during the First World War, the company emerged with two unscathed vessels. Oddly enough in 1924 a huge investment was made and five brand new vessels were delivered. They were the *Amblestone* (6095 gross tons), *Coniston* (6097 gross tons), *Rochdale* (6098 gross tons), *Snowdon* (5205 gross tons) and *Overstone* (5204 gross tons). The only other vessel they possessed was the 1898 built, 2974 gross ton steamer, the *Reresby*. In July, 1926 Charles Radcliffe died and with his death a highly successful company was wound up.

Charles Radcliffe

The first Snowdon, *pictured in the Bay of Naples*

21

Care and Marquand

Hilary Blondel Marquand, like the Hacquoil Brothers and Thomas and Philip Morel, was a native of the Channel Islands and he left his native Guernsey in the 1870s for Cardiff. For some time he worked with an uncle who was already settled in the port as a coal exporter, but soon he was in business with W.H. Martin, an established tug owner at the port, whose single vessel was the wooden steam tug *Princess*. The new company, trading as Martin and Marquand, developed very rapidly and by 1894 they owned six vessels, three of which were typical tramp steamers of their day, the *Earl of Dumfries, Earl of Roseberry* and the *Rosehill*. The other three vessels were the steam paddle tugs run by W.H. Martin, namely *Earl of Bute, Earl of Dunraven* and *Earl of Jersey*. As time progressed Martin and Marquand invested in larger ships so that by the outbreak of the First World War they operated three steamers of over 2,000 tons each, the *Dauntless, Relentless* and *Silvia*. The company continued to trade until the early 1920s although by that time the Marquand family were associated with a number of other prominent Cardiff docks people, the most notable being the Care family. Care and Marquand became an important shipping company and the Cares themselves had long been associated with Cardiff being owners of the Deansgate Steamship Company (Care and Perry) of the early 1900s and the Vindomura Shipping Company of the same period. Both these companies were operators of small coastal steamers, the *Porthleven* of 342 tons and the *Vindomura* of 600 tons.

The Care family were natives of Cardiff and from the late nineteenth century until the 1960s they were to contribute a great deal to the economic affairs of the port. Richard Care was in business as early as 1894 with a single ship company running the *Vindomura*. By 1913 the company ran the 1,114 ton *Jeanie*. His son Edward Richard Care was a consulting marine engineer who, in the early 1920s with his friend Leonard Marquand, set up business in Cardiff purchasing three tramp steamers – *Arncliffe, Beachcliffe* and *Coniscliffe*, vessels that were principally used in the South American trade. In the meantime, another Care, Edward's brother Richard Penberthy Care, established another company which, in 1920, ran the small 300 ton *Nuola*. Care Lines were to continue in business until 1955 operating no more than two small steamers at any one time. All their vessels had the prefix *Porth* – *Porthmorna* (592 tons), *Porthmeor* (449 tons) and *Porthrepta* (643 tons). In 1955, just before the demise of the company, two single ship companies – Care Lines Ltd. and R.P. Care, the one running the *Porthrepta* and the other the 752 ton *Carbis Bay*, were operated.

Hilary Blondel Marquand left his native Guernsey for Cardiff in the 1870s

The Earl of Dumfries *was built for Martin & Marquand in 1882*

Leonard Marquand

The Coniscliffe *was a standard government war-time vessel, built in 1918 as the* War Anglian

The Porthrepta *was operated by Care Lines until the mid 1950s*

The W. & C.T. Jones Steamship Co. Ltd.

Whereas the majority of those who participated in Cardiff's golden era as a coal-exporting port were immigrants to the city, coming from all parts of the British Isles and further afield, William Jones, the founder of W. & C.T. Jones, was a native of Cardiff, born in 1838 a year before Cardiff's first dock facility was completed. Little is known of his early life other than that he went to sea when still very young, but in 1884 he set up the Cymmrodorion Steamship Co. Ltd. to acquire and operate the vessel of that name then being built on the Tyne. Four years later there followed the *Kate B. Jones,* and by the turn of the century, William Jones was the managing owner of nine steel tramp steamers, each registered as single ship companies. Four of these vessels bore names with the Welsh suffix '-*wen*', meaning white, and in later years most of the company's vessels were to bear Welsh names with this suffix.

In 1902, the decision was taken to form a single joint-stock limited company in place of the nine single-ship companies then in existence. The W. & C.T. Jones Steamship Co. Ltd. was incorporated on 14th July that year, with a capital of £280,000 in £1 shares; among the earliest subscribers to the firm was Edward Nicholl, later to become a shipowner himself, but at that time marine superintendent to William Jones's newly established enterprise. The new firm soon showed itself to be a phenomenally successful venture; during 1908, which was one of the worst years of the depression of 1904-1911, it made a profit of almost £30,000, whereas in 1913 a profit of over £111,000 was made. The firm continued to do very well during the early years of the First World War, but latterly the effects of the Excess Profits Duty hit the company very badly and in 1918 it was decided that the firm should be wound up. Most of the vessels were sold for a good price during the immediate post-war boom, and the firm was eventually wound up in September 1924.

William Jones, founder of W. & C.T. Jones

The new Pontwen *on trials off Hartlepool in 1914*

24

P. & A. Campbell – the 'White Funnel' Fleet

Captain Daniel Jenkins with crew members aboard the Pontwen *in 1917*

The Nantwen *was completed for W. & C.T. Jones at Stockton-on-Tees in 1912*

Although it was not until the late 1950s that the firm of P. & A. Campbell transferred its offices to Cardiff, the company's passenger steamers with their distinctive white funnels were an integral part of the Cardiff dockland scene from the late 1880s, when the brothers Peter and Alec Campbell moved from the Clyde to a new base at Bristol. The Campbell family had been involved with passenger steamers on the Clyde since the 1850s, but it was in 1893 that the limited company of P. & A. Campbell was formed, owning the two paddle steamers, *Waverley* and *Ravenswood.* The initial success of their operations in the Bristol Channel led the firm to acquire a further three new vessels by 1896, though they were in competition with other locally owned steamers, such as those run by the Cardiff shipowner John Gunn.

P. & A. Campbell's most serious competitors in the Bristol Channel, however, were the three vessels bought by the Barry Railway Co. from 1905 onwards as they attempted to diversify their interests and encourage regular passenger services and tourist excursions from Barry. So concerned were the Campbell brothers that they took the Barry Railway Co. to court, where they were so successful in restricting the latter's operations that they disposed of their fine new vessels in 1910. A year later, these vessels were bought by P. & A. Campbell and integrated into their fleet.

During the First World War, the company's services were severely restricted as their vessels were commissioned as minesweepers. Three of them were lost, though when in 1915, the Admiralty began to order purpose-built paddle minesweepers, they based their design on Campbell's P.S.*Glen Usk,* thus creating the 'Racecourse' class of minesweepers. After the war, the company revived its regular and excursion services in the Bristol Channel, and it also ran extensive operations on the south coast, chiefly from Brighton, from 1923 onwards. The inter-war years, however, also saw the deaths of the founding partners; Alec Campbell died at his native Kilmun in 1928, while his brother Peter passed away ten years later at Bristol.

During the Second World War, Campbell's steamers once more distinguished themselves, with the paddle steamers *Brighton Belle, Devonia* and *Brighton Queen* all being lost during the Dunkirk evacuations in 1940. Together with other Campbell steamers present at that time, they rescued over 7,000 troops. Following the war, they had two new paddle steamers built; the *Bristol Queen* of 1946 and the *Cardiff Queen* of 1947. Post-war economic conditions were not favourable to the firm; the older steamers were scrapped and in 1959, a receiver was appointed. The firm was rescued, however, by the intervention of Sydney Smith-Cox who drew the attention of Roland Wickenden of Townsend Car Ferries to P. & A. Campbell. His backing enabled the firm to resume operations for the 1960 season, and in 1963, they experimented with a hovercraft service from Penarth to Weston. By 1979, however, the situation was once more critical, with poor passenger figures and falling receipts. Shortly afterwards, they ceased trading, but the tradition of passenger excursion vessels in the Bristol Channel has been maintained in the 1980s by the preserved paddle steamer *Waverley* and more recently by a former Campbell motor vessel, the *Balmoral*.

Campbell's landing stages at the Pierhead in Butetown

*Captain Alexander Campbell, one of the
co-founders of P. & A. Campbell*

Ilfracombe was a popular destination for summer excursions operated from Cardiff by P. & A. Campbell

The Westward Ho! *in service as a minesweeper during the First World War*

The immaculate engine room of the Devonia

The Cambria *crowded with passengers*

The Cardiff Queen *laid up at Penarth dock in the 1960s*

John Mathias & Sons, Aberystwyth and Cardiff

John Mathias was born at Llanbadarn Fawr near Aberystwyth in 1837 and by 1860, he was running a grocery shop at 7, Bridge Street, Aberystwyth. Prior to the arrival of the railway in the town in 1864, much of the merchandise that grocers like John Mathias retailed would have reached Aberystwyth by sea, and he held shares in a number of locally owned sailing vessels. By 1876, he was the registered owner of two coastal sailing vessels, but with the trade of the local port declining through the competition of an increasingly efficient railway system, he set up the Glanrheidol Steamship Co. in October 1883 to acquire and operate the iron tramp steamer of that name. At 1,005 gross tons, she was far too big to enter Aberystwyth and she was bought specifically to participate in the coal trade out of Cardiff. Over the next ten years, John Mathias acquired a further five steamers, all named with the prefix 'Glan-' and all registered as single ship companies. Among the prominent shareholders in these early companies were the Rev. Thomas Levi, minister of the Tabernacl Calvinistic Methodist Chapel in Aberystwyth where Mathias was a deacon, and Thomas Charles Edwards, first Principal of the college at Aberystwyth.

It was in October 1896 that the Cambrian Steam Navigation Co. was set up, initially as a single-ship company. By 1905, however, all the other companies managed by Mathias had been wound up and their assets transferred to the latter company to form a single joint-stock venture. By this date, John Mathias's second son Richard was running a second office at Cardiff in addition to the registered office at Aberystwyth and the firm also began to name its vessels after public schools in England and Wales, thus earning it the nickname in Cardiff of 'the College line'. To the many seamen from Aberystwyth and Borth who served with the firm, however, John Mathias's vessels were always *llongau Aberystwyth* − the ships of Aberystwyth. John Mathias died in 1912, and the firm was taken over by Richard Mathias who had trained as a barrister. Knighted in 1913 and made a baronet in 1917, Sir Richard Mathias managed the company through the years of the war when three ships were lost through enemy action. They disposed of their last vessel, a standard First World War steamer, the *Western,* in 1922, just as the great slump that undermined Cardiff's immediate post-war boom began to make its effects felt, and the Cambrian Steam Navigation Co. was finally wound up in December 1924.

| Thomas Owens. | Evan Evans. | James Warrell. | John Mathias. | Ebenezer Morgan. | John Jenkins. |
| R. K. Humphreys. | Y Parch. William Jones. | Y Parch. Thomas Levi. | | Y Parch. John Williams. | John Lloyd. |

The deacons of the Tabernacl Calvinistic Methodist Chapel, Aberystwyth in 1900. John Mathias is the third on the right in the back row

The harbour at Aberystwyth in 1860

A view forward from the poop on board the Glanhafren. (E.N. Taylor)

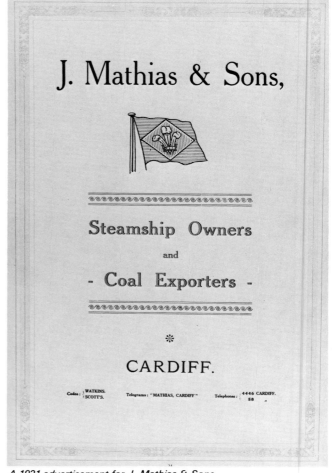

J. Mathias & Sons,

Steamship Owners

and

- Coal Exporters -

CARDIFF.

Codes: WATKINS. SCOTT'S.   Telegrams: "MATHIAS, CARDIFF"   Telephones: 4446 CARDIFF. 56

A 1921 advertisement for J. Mathias & Sons

The Etonian *of 1901, seen at Amsterdam in 1906. (K. O'Donoghue collection)*

An artist's impression of the Southern *in a North Atlantic storm*

Turnbull Bros.

The port of Whitby on the north Yorkshire coast has a long tradition of maritime associations ranging from fishing to shipowning and ship-building. Pre-eminent among the town's maritime families were the Turnbulls who were involved in shipping from at least the early eighteenth century and at whose Whitby yard numerous stoutly-built collier brigs and barques were constructed. From 1871 onwards, the Turnbulls built steamers for their own fleet at Whitby and six years later, the brothers Philip and Lewis Turnbull moved from Whitby to Cardiff, initially to act as chartering agents at the expanding coal port for the fleet of steamers operated by their father, Thomas Turnbull.

In 1882, the Turnbull brothers entered shipowning on their own account with the purchase of the iron tramp steamer *Everilda* of 1,455 gross tons, followed by the *Gwendoline* of 1833 and the *Bernard* of 1884. By 1900 they had a fleet of eight steamers, all of which had been built by the parent company at Whitby, though shipbuilding at the Yorkshire port was destined to cease after 1902 owing to the limitations placed upon the beam of new vessels by the bridge over the River Esk at Whitby through which all new ships had to pass. Thereafter the Turnbull brothers had to turn to outside builders to supply them with new vessels. Until 1910, moreover, the brothers had continued a policy of dividing their vessels into traditional 64th shares, but in that year they established a single joint-stock limited company named 'Turnbull Bros. Shipping Co. Ltd.'. A year later, they set up a further company, the Horngarth Shipping Co. Ltd. to acquire and operate the S.S. *Horngarth* built by Thompsons of Sunderland in 1911; she was one of the seven vessels managed by the Turnbull brothers on the eve of the First World War.

Six vessels were lost during the ensuing hostilities and the end of the war saw the firm left with two vessels only, the *Collingham* acquired in 1910 and the *Ruel,* built new for the firm in 1917. Foreseeing that Cardiff's post-war boom would be followed by a slump, both vessels were sold for a handsome price in 1919 and a year later the Turnbull brothers wound up the Cardiff firm. In 1921, however, Lewis Turnbull's sons Cyril and Bertrand set up Turnbull's (Cardiff) Ltd. to act as chartering agents at Cardiff for Turnbull, Scott & Co. of London. Re-enacting the careers of their father and uncle, they too entered into shipowning in 1924 as the Turnbull Coal & Shipping Co. Ltd. and by 1927 they owned three tramp steamers at Cardiff. The depressed conditions of the 1930s, however, persuaded the partners to dispose of their last vessel in 1937, though they remained in business as agents and ship-brokers in Cardiff until 1943.

Philip Turnbull, co-founder with his brother Lewis, of Turnbull Bros., Cardiff

The Turnbull's shipyard on the River Esk at Whitby. (Courtesy of the Sutcliffe Gallery, Whitby)

The Bernard, *built at Whitby in 1884*

Neale and West

Joshua John Neale was born in Ireland of English parents and with his cycling friend Henry West of Bristol they established a fish merchants' business in Custom House Street in Cardiff in 1885. The fish they sold came from other ports, but they persuaded some of the Cardiff tugmasters to take trawl nets on board their vessels while seeking tows in the Bristol Channel. Supplies were irregular and in 1888 the fish merchants decided to purchase the 52-ton trawler *Lark* from a Hull fishing company. The company flourished and by 1906 they owned a fleet of 19 trawlers based on the Bute West Dock. From 1907 they were also concerned with fishing operations from Milford Haven.

Henry West left the company in 1910 and it was operated by J.J. Neale and his seven sons. J.J. Neale became friendly with Japanese businessmen and Neale and West were responsible for training Japanese fishermen in the art of trawling. As a result of this connection, it became the custom for Neale and West to give their steam trawlers Japanese names — the *Fuji, Nodzu, Kuroki* and *Oku.*

During the First World War the whole fleet was recruited for mine-sweeping duties and at the end of hostilities the company were left with a greatly depleted fleet. That fleet was completely modernised in the 1920s and '30s with modern trawlers of 300 gross tons; these vessels were purchased from shipyards in Selby, Middlesborough and elsewhere. The *Kunisti* of 1927, for example, was built at Smith's Dock, Middlesborough and was a vessel of 303 gross tons, 130 feet long, 24 feet wide and had a draught of 12 feet. The whole fleet was concerned principally with fishing off the south and west coasts of Ireland. Nevertheless, those fishing grounds, especially the hake supply, were becoming over-fished and by 1939 the Cardiff as well as the Milford trawling fleets were no longer very lucrative. Fish stocks did recover slightly after 1945, but the industry soon fell on bad times again. By the early 1950s, the hake grounds had become almost exhausted and Neale and West were experiencing great difficulty in recruiting suitable staff. The trawlers themselves had to sail further and further from their home port in search of fish although vessels were not large enough to sail to distant Arctic waters to fish. Neither were they modern enough, for at the end of the Second World War, Neale and West attempted to replace the vessels lost during the war with second-hand tonnage, built in the 1920s and used for many years by Hull and Grimsby trawlermen. In 1956 all fishing operations ceased, and that year saw the end of Cardiff as a fishing port of any consequence and trawlers no longer came to the quayside at the West Bute Dock as they had done for over sixty years.

The Hamdale, *acquired by the Turnbull Coal and Shipping Co. in 1924.* (*World Ship Photo Library*)

*Joshua John Neale, co-founder of Neale & West.
(J.K. Neale Collection)*

The Oku *enters the West Bute Basin, Cardiff on 6 June 1930. (J.K. Neale Collection)*

The Akita *returning from her maiden voyage on 18 June 1939.
(J.K. Neale Collection)*

The cod-end is opened aboard the Iwate *on 2 April 1946. (J.K. Neale Collection)*

The deck hands have almost finished gutting the catch aboard the Iwate *in April 1946. (J.K. Neale Collection)*

Discharging and weighing the catch alongside the West Bute Basin, April 1930. (J.K. Neale Collection)

Part of the Neale & West lorry fleet in March 1934. (J.K. Neale Collection)

W.J. Tatem and The Tatem Steam Navigation Co. Ltd.

William James Tatem was born in Appledore, Devon in 1868 and after a brief period serving on board various vessels out of that port, moved to Cardiff shortly after his eighteenth birthday. There, he obtained employment as a clerk in the offices of another shipping family of Appledore origins, Anning Bros., and his many years' service in the firm's office made him thoroughly conversant with all aspects of tramp ship management.

He decided to enter into shipping on his own account in 1897 with the creation of the Lady Lewis Steamship Co. Ltd. incorporated to acquire the new steamer of that name under construction at Stockton-on-Tees. Another former employee of Anning Bros., William Reardon Smith, was appointed master of the vessel, which was the first of 16 acquired over the succeeding eight years. In 1905, he acquired two large turret-decked vessels, which were at that time the largest steamers owned at Cardiff, and five years later in 1910, the 14 vessels then in the fleet were all transferred to the newly formed Tatem Steam Navigation Co. Ltd.. On the eve of the First World War, this company operated a fine fleet of 16 relatively new tramp steamers.

W.J. Tatem was knighted in 1916, and in 1918 he was created 1st Baron Glanely of St. Fagans in recognition of his contribution to the war effort. Following the war, he took advantage of the boom of 1919-20 by selling off at a high price all eight vessels that had survived the hostilities. In their place, a fleet of six new vessels was acquired that were better suited to survive the economic difficulties of the 1920s. Further vessels were added in the late 1920s, and shareholders in the Tatem fleet were rewarded with consistently high dividends throughout the depressed 1920s and '30s as a result of Lord Glanely's commercial foresight. Apart from his shipping interests, Lord Glanely's other great love was horse racing; he owned an extensive stable near his Newmarket house, and horses from his stable won all five Classic races.

Lord Glanely was killed tragically during a bombing raid on Weston-super-Mare in 1942, and at the end of the Second World War, the firm possessed four vessels. With the decline of the coal trade from South Wales, these ships were employed tramping world-wide under the management of Lord Glanely's nephew, G.C. Gibson. In 1960, the firm moved its offices from Cardiff to London and five years later, they acquired what was to be their last vessel, the *Exning*. This vessel was eventually disposed of in 1973, though the firm continues in existence today as an investment company in London.

W.J. Tatem, 1st Baron Glanely of St. Fagans

Tatem's second vessel was the Sir W.T. Lewis *of 1898*

The Torrington *was one of two turret-decked vessels completed for Tatem in 1905; at the time, they were the largest ships owned at Cardiff, with a capacity of 9,000 deadweight tons*

The turbine steamer Lord Glanely *was completed at Sunderland in 1947*

Lord Glanely leading in 'Singapore', victorious in the St. Leger in 1930

'Exning', Tatem's house at Newmarket

Owen & Watkin Williams — 'Llongau Pwllparc'

The brothers Owen and Watkin Williams were born and brought up at Pwllparc farm near Edern in the Llŷn Peninsula, and were to be among the foremost of Cardiff's shipowners during the first decade of the present century. Both first went to sea aboard the coastal trading vessels of the North Wales ports, but by the 1890s they were experienced masters in steam, Watkin Williams, for instance, serving as master on the Elder Dempster steamer *Memphis* from 1893 onwards. Both retired from active seafaring in the late 1890s and in 1899 they set up the Silurian Steamship Co. Ltd. at Cardiff to acquire and operate the 940 gross ton steamer of that name. By 1905, they were operating nine tramp steamers, many of which were relatively small vessels that traded chiefly to the Bay of Biscay and the western Mediterranean. As was the case with many of the Welsh-founded Cardiff shipping companies, Owen and Watkin Williams employed a large number of mariners from their native area on their vessels, and the firm's ships were known to these North Walian mariners as *'Llongau Pwllparc'* — the ships of Pwllparc.

In 1900, the partners established a new shipping venture known as 'The Golden Cross Line'; three of their vessels were later registered in this company's name and unusually for Cardiff owners, the new company was set up specifically to maintain a cargo liner service from Liverpool, Swansea, Bristol and Cardiff to Mediterranean ports such as Barcelona, Marseilles, Genoa and Livorno. On the eve of the First World War, they were operating a total of ten vessels, some of which maintained the liner service while the remainder participated in Cardiff's traditional tramping trades to the Black Sea and the River Plate. Four of these vessels were lost through enemy action during the ensuing hostilities and by 1921 the firm's fleet was further reduced to two vessels as a result of post-war sales.

In 1923, the firm (by now under the sole management of Owen Williams) took a bold step when they built one of the first Cardiff-owned motor vessels, the *Margretian* of 2,578 gross tons, followed a year later by her larger sister ship, the *Silurian*. With ample supplies of steam coal available, Cardiff owners were sceptical about diesel-powered vessels, and their scepticism was borne out in their observations of the experiences of Owen Williams. Both vessels proved to be complete failures and the firm soon found itself in very difficult financial circumstances, compounded by large losses sustained by the Mediterranean liner services. The two remaining steamers were sold in 1925, and in 1929 the firm was forced to dispose of its last vessel, the *Margretian* (which had been laid up at Cardiff since 1925), for less than a tenth of her building price of over

£140,000. In all, the company had run up losses in excess of £400,000 between 1923 and 1930 and the entire venture was wound up in April and May, 1930, thus bringing to an end a daring experiment that had manifestly failed to prove a commercial success.

Captain Owen Williams

Captain Watkin Williams in his dress as High Sheriff of Caernarfonshire in 1930-31

An advertisement for the Golden Cross Line's services dating from 1921

The Arvonian, *built for Owen and Watkin Williams at Stockton-on-Tees in 1905. This vessel saw service as a 'Q-ship' during the First World War*

The ill-fated Margretian *of 1923. (E.N. Taylor)*

W.E. Hinde

W.E. Hinde was born in 1877 at Portland, Dorset, where his father was a shopkeeper. In 1893, however, the young William moved to Cardiff to take up a post in the offices of Messrs. Chellew & Co., a Truro-based tramp-shipping firm who operated many of their Falmouth-registered steamers in the coal trade out of Cardiff. He remained in Chellew's Cardiff office for ten years, during which period he became thoroughly conversant with all aspects of tramp-shipping management.

Having left Chellew's in 1903 William Hinde entered into partnership with Captain Robert McNiel to form the company of McNiel, Hinde & Co. and in that year they acquired a new steamship of 2,793 gross tons, the *Portland*. She was followed by the *Portsmouth* in 1906 and the *Portreath* in 1907. By 1914, the two other vessels had been sold, and the fleet consisted of two steamers, the *Portreath* and the *Portloe*, built in 1912. On the eve of the war, however, Hinde dissolved his partnership with Captain McNiel and established himself as W.E. Hinde & Co.

The firm suffered a number of losses during the years of the war, including that of the *Portloe*, torpedoed 160 miles WNW. of the Fastnet light on 20 April, 1917; 24 of her crew, including the master, were lost in this tragic incident. In place of the lost vessels, a number of second-hand steamers were purchased during the latter years of the war; in 1918, for instance, Hinde acquired the former Strick steamer, *Nigaristan* and the former Seager vessel, *Amicus*. These vessels were respectively re-named *Portloe* and *Portreath*. W.E. Hinde was also involved in other branches of the shipping industry in Cardiff and further afield; in July 1916 he established the Cardiff Ship Store Co. Ltd., a chandlery business in Butetown, and he was also active on the boards of various bodies concerned with the regulation of the shipping industry and shipping insurance.

Following the cessation of hostilities, W.E. Hinde augmented his fleet with further modern steamers such as the *Portfield* of 1919, the *Portgwarra*, bought in 1922, and the *Portcurno* of 1924. He continued to trade this substantial fleet throughout the difficult years of the 1920s; realising that to trade successfully in the depressed conditions of that time it was necessary to employ modern up-to-date vessels, Hinde continued to invest in new steamers such as the second *Portfield* of 1929 and the *Portregis* of 1930. However, the difficult economic conditions prevailing at the time soon began to have an adverse effect upon Hinde's shipping ventures; a balance sheet of July 1931 recorded losses in excess of £26,000 and some of the steamers had been laid up for

considerable periods of time. In December 1931, the *Portloe* was sold in an effort to improve the firm's liquidity, but the company eventually folded with W.E. Hinde's bankruptcy in 1932.

W.E. Hinde

The launch of the Portreath *from the shipyard of J. Blumer & Co., Sunderland in 1907*

The completed Portreath *carrying a deck cargo of timber*

The Portfield, *launched in 1929, was one of the last vessels built for W.E. Hinde & Co.*

J.T. Duncan

John Thomas Duncan was never in the forefront of Cardiff shipowners. His business, established in 1889 and continuing until 1960, always depended on small steamers, many of them bought on the second-hand market that were expected to last the company a long time. Thus the *Maywood,* an 1,800 gross ton steamer, was built by a Tyneside shipyard in 1922 and was purchased by Duncan in 1930. With her tall, thin black funnel the vessel was to remain in the fleet until the demise of the company in 1960.

Throughout the seventy year history of the company, the ships were mainly concerned with taking coal out of the South Wales ports, especially from Penarth to the Bay of Biscay, the Iberian Peninsula and North Africa. They were also concerned with the coaling of Royal Navy ships at Scapa Flow and other naval stations in the British Isles. Those vessels on voyages to North Africa and south-west Europe brought back pit-props and esparto grass for the paper industry.

The company trading as Duncan, Valette and Co. with its offices at 95 James Street, Cardiff, was established in 1889 and the Liverpool-built vessel of 1880, the *Benefactor* of 1,034 gross tons, was purchased for use in the coal trade. By 1895, J.T. Duncan was a shipowner in his own right operating the *Benefactor* until 1898 and purchasing the 15 year-old steamer *Stokesay* of 1,038 gross tons in 1895. The latter was to have a particularly long life, for although she was sold by Duncan in 1912, when already 32 years-old, she sailed the seas as a Swedish vessel until 1951.

Little is known about Duncan himself, but he was obviously a man with considerable engineering expertise as well as a minor shipowner. In 1907 he patented a system of 'improving the construction of screw propelled vessels' by fitting water-tight tanks over and on the sides of the propeller shafts of vessels, thus increasing their cargo carrying capabilities. Unlike most of his contemporaries Duncan advocated a pattern of ship design which placed machinery aft, as found in most cargo vessels today. To prove his point, in 1912 he ordered two vessels, with machinery and funnel aft from Clydeside shipbuilders — the *Agnes Duncan* and *Ellie Duncan* of 2,500 gross tons. In 1914 all was well with the company despite losing one of its larger vessels, the *J.Duncan,* off the treacherous Cornish coast and at the outbreak of the First World War, five vessels were owned by the company, including a brand new flagship — the second *J.Duncan,* built by a Dublin shipyard in 1914. In 1920 they still owned three vessels, for the war had been kinder to Duncan than most of his Cardiff contemporaries.

In the 1920s, the fleet of slightly elderly vessels still sailed on to be joined in 1930 by an eight year-old vessel named the *Maywood* of 1,823 gross tons. By the mid 1950s cargoes were becoming far more difficult to find especially for a small, old steamer like the *Maywood,* the only ship now owned by the company. For two years she was laid up at Penarth Dock, but in November 1959 she was sold to a Belgian shipbreaker and the history of one of the smaller Cardiff shipowning companies came to an end.

An almost identical successor, the second J. Duncan *was built in 1914*

The first J. Duncan *was wrecked at Tolpedn on the Cornish coast in August 1913*

The Agnes Duncan *at Algiers in 1925*

Jenkins Bros.

The village of Aber-porth on the coast of southern Ceredigion has a long and fascinating heritage of maritime associations, not the least of these being the four Cardiff tramp-shipping firms set up by master mariners from the village around the turn of the nineteenth century. Captain Evan Thomas of Aber-porth was one of the founding partners of Evan Thomas, Radcliffe & Co. in Cardiff in 1881, and among the master mariners from Aber-porth employed by the firm in the 1890s were the brothers-in-law James and David Jenkins. Their families had long been involved in the village's busy coastal trade owning the smacks *Mary Anne* and *James,* but in 1897, James Jenkins set up the Gathorne Steamship Co. to acquire and operate the 1873-built tramp steamer of that name. Joined in 1898-9 by his brother-in-law and W.J. Williams of Bethesda, Gwynedd, the partnership was managing a total of seven second-hand vessels by 1900.

W.J. Williams left the partnership in October 1904 and thereafter James and David Jenkins traded under the name of Jenkins Bros.; in 1906 they bought their first new tramp steamer, the *Glamorgan* and she was followed a year later by the trunk-decked *Cardigan,* built by Ropner's of Stockton-on-Tees. On the eve of the First World War, they were managing five vessels, all but one of which were lost or disposed of during the ensuing hostilities. Following the sudden death of David Jenkins in November 1919, the company's affairs were rationalised with the winding up of many of the defunct single-ship companies and the sale of the remaining vessels. In 1923, however, a new company, the Cardigan Shipping Co., was set up by James Jenkins and two new steamers, the *Radnor* and the *Merioneth,* were acquired by the firm in 1923-4. These ships traded quite successfully during the difficult years of the mid-1920s, but in 1927, James Jenkins (then aged 67) decided to retire from shipowning and both vessels were sold to Morels of Cardiff. The Cardigan Shipping Co., however, continued to trade and still remains in existence today, jointly managed by Glasgow and Oslo-based shipping concerns. Bearing in mind the origins of the firm, it is appropriate that one of the modern bulk carriers that the company presently possesses, the *Norse Marshal,* is registered at Cardiff.

James Jenkins

The Jenkinses first entered into shipping in the coasting trade of south-west Wales, with vessels such as these smacks seen at Aber-porth, c.1885

The Italiana *taking on a cargo of coal at Penarth in October 1910*

Edward Nicholl and the Cardiff 'Hall' Line

Edward Nicholl was born in Redruth, Cornwall in 1862, and began his career as an apprentice engineer in the Great Western Railway works at Swindon under the famous Sir Daniel Gooch. He first came to South Wales in 1883 as foreman of a Newport ship-repairing yard, but a year later he became chief engineer on board Evan Thomas, Radcliffe's first vessel, *Gwenllian Thomas,* the youngest man ever to hold such a post on a Cardiff vessel. He became the firm's marine superintendent and later served in a similar capacity with another well-known Cardiff firm, W. & C.T. Jones.

In 1903, he decided to venture into shipowning on his own account and during the following year he set up companies to acquire two new turret-decked steamers, the first ever owned at Cardiff. This gave rise to considerable comment among the port's more conservative shipowners, but the astounding success of the venture more than justified Nicholl's faith in the turret design. Within two years of the establishment of the firm, his vessels had made profits of between 20% and 25% per annum, while, between July 1904 and October 1905, the *Whateley Hall* made a total profit in excess of £6,000. He was described in January 1906 by the Cardiff-based *Maritime Review* as, '. . . one of Cardiff's youngest and certainly the most phenomenally successful steamer managers', and by the eve of the First World War, he was the managing owner of a fleet of ten up-to-date vessels. During the war, however, he became a fierce critic of the Excess Profits Duty that drastically reduced the profits of so many shipowners, so much so that he disposed of his entire fleet in 1917 to the Cardiff-Norwegian Sven Hansen. Thereafter, he only briefly re-entered shipowning in 1929-32; having been knighted in 1916, he was elected Tory M.P. for Penryn and Falmouth in 1919 and he was also very active with the Royal Naval Reserve. He died in London in 1939.

The Radnor *on pre-delivery trials in July 1923*

Sir Edward Nicholl, photographed in 1903 as he was embarking upon his career as a shipowner

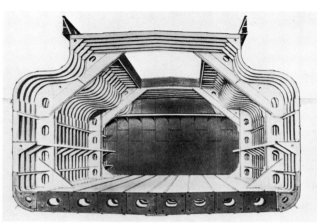

A cross-section of a turret-decked vessel. Nicholl was the first Cardiff owner to invest in these vessels

Nicholl's close associations with the Royal Naval Reserve led to the adoption of a naval-style uniform for the sailors that served on his steamers

The Grindon Hall, *built in 1905, was lost without trace in December 1907 while bound from Sulina to Glasgow with a cargo of maize and barley*

W.H. Seager & Co. – the Tempus Shipping Company Ltd.

William Henry Seager was born in Cardiff in 1862 the son of William and Mary Jane Seager of Ilfracombe who moved to South Wales in the 1850s. William Seager was a builder and he was attracted to Cardiff by the great expansion of the port in the mid-nineteenth century. Unfortunately, his health deteriorated and he was bedridden for 30 years with the result that his son could not become an architect as he wished but had to find work at an early age. In 1885 he obtained work at a wage of 4 shillings a week in a Cardiff ship chandlery. In 1892 he became a ship chandler himself, establishing his business at 109 Bute Street. Ship chandlers were often in privileged positions and many, such as Joseph Frazer, invested very heavily in Cardiff shipowning companies though only a few possessed ships of their own. Seager, however, in 1904 purchased a brand new vessel of 2,981 gross tons from the Stockton yard of Craig Taylor, registered in the name of W.H. Seager & Co. This vessel, the *Tempus*, remained the only vessel in the company's fleet for five years. Most of the shares in the new shipping company were owned by Seager himself but among the minor shareholders were William Reardon Smith who was destined to become one of the largest Cardiff shipowners.

The fleet was gradually expanded and new ships such as the *Amicus* in 1910 and second-hand vessels such as the *Starcross* (renamed *Virtus*), the *Margaret Jones* (renamed *Beatus*) and the *Loyal Briton* (renamed *Salvus*) were added to the fleet. Despite disposing of some vessels, the Seager fleet of 1914 consisted of four vessels all less than ten years old – *Tempus* (2,891 tons), *Amicus* (3,695 tons), *Salvus* (2,259 tons) and *Campus* (3,054 tons). Unlike many other Cardiff shipowners, W.H. Seager never invested in new ships in the boom years immediately following the First World War; indeed, he sold three of his vessels to other shipowners at a substantial price. In 1924 trade was recovering slightly and Seager built three new vessels – *Amicus*, *Campus* and *Beatus* and by 1928 they owned 7 vessels. During the Second World War they managed a number of ships for the Shipping Controller, but all their vessels except the *Campus* of 1928 were sunk by enemy action. Two more standard war-time vessels – *Amicus* (7,125 tons) and *Beatus* (7,442 tons) were provided in 1946-7, but the *Beatus* was sold in 1955 leaving the *Amicus* as the last vessel in the fleet. In 1963, the business was wound up.

William Henry Seager was an important figure in Cardiff's dockland; he served as Liberal M.P. for Cardiff East from 1918 to 1922 and was knighted in 1918. His sons, John Elliot Seager (1891-1955) and George Leighton Seager (1896-1963) (created Baron Leighton of St. Mellons in 1962) were directors of the shipping company and were both prominent in the public life of South Wales.

Sir William Seager

The Amicus *sailing into Cardiff in 1936*

The Beatus *at Cardiff in 1952*

The doorstep of Seager's Buildings in Bute Street

The Reardon Smith Line

William Reardon Smith was born of a seafaring family at Appledore, Devon, in 1856, and at the age of twelve, he went to sea on board the local sloop *Unity*. During the following years he served on board a number of local vessels and having acquired his First Mate's certificate in 1878, joined the well-known company Hogarth's of Ardrossan. A year later he gained his Master's certificate in 1881, at the age of 25, took command of Hogarth's barque *Drumadoon*. He remained with the company (having latterly commanded a number of their steamers) until 1896, when he became master of the *Starcross* owned by Anning Bros. of Cardiff, who were also of Appledore origins. A year later, another Appledore-born Cardiff shipowner, W.J. Tatem, invited him to command his first steamer, the *Lady Lewis* and he subsequently commanded Tatem's *Shandon* before retiring from active sea-faring and settling in Cardiff in 1900.

Having initially made numerous investments in property and shipping in Cardiff, William Reardon Smith ventured into shipowning in 1905 with the ordering of the *City of Cardiff* from Ropner's of Stockton-on-Tees. Delivered a year later, she was followed by further vessels so that by 1914 the firm possessed a fleet of nine modern tramp steamers. All bore names with the 'City' suffix and though owned at Cardiff, they were all registered at Bideford, being the port of registry of the founder's home town of Appledore. Despite losses, the firm expanded during the war years; in 1917, eight vessels formerly belonging to Pyman Bros. of London were added to the fleet and despite the high cost of tonnage during the immediate post-war boom, twelve further vessels were acquired from various sources in 1919.

Elevated to a baronetcy in 1920 in recognition of his contribution to the war effort, Sir William Reardon Smith realised that with the decline of the South Wales coal trade, it would be better to concentrate the activities of his fleet in the world-wide tramping trades. By 1922 he controlled 39 vessels and in 1928 a cargo liner service to the Pacific ports of North America was inaugurated. 1928 also saw the purchase of the firm's first motor vessels, the *East Lynn* and *West Lynn*. With its policy of trading world-wide, the firm rode out the vicissitudes of the 1930s quite well, though some of its vessels spent periods laid up on the River Fal and poor returns on the liner trade led to its demise in 1937. The 1930s also saw the death of Sir William Reardon Smith who died in his eightieth year in December 1935; a generous benefactor of the National Museum of Wales, he was succeeded by his son, Sir Willie Reardon Smith, who also took over the chairmanship of the firm.

20 Reardon Smith vessels were lost through enemy action during the Second World War. During the post-war years, the firm continued to participate in the world-wide tramping trade with a fleet of some 20 vessels, but with the downward trend evident in the shipping market by the late 1950s, the directors began to consider the future needs of the firm with regard to new vessels. The last conventional tramp-style vessel built for the firm was the *Houston City* of 1963 and during the following year they acquired their first bulk carrier with engines and accommodation aft, the *Australian City*. Thereafter all new vessels built for the firm were of this design, including the 'Cardiff' class of bulk carriers built by Upper Clyde Shipbuilders in the early 1970s. From 1972 onwards, the company began to manage vessels on behalf of the Mexican Transportacion Maritima Mexicana S.A. and in 1973-4, further extended its interests, firstly with the creation of a shipping pool named Celtic Bulk Carriers in association with Irish Shipping Ltd. and secondly by acquiring a 28% interest in an oil exploration firm, the Atlantic Drilling Co. Ltd.

From the mid-1970s onwards, however, the worsening state of the world freight market had a critical effect upon the Reardon Smith Line. Numerous vessels were sold and in 1978 the firm relinquished its oil exploration interests in an effort to reduce its liabilities. By 1984 its own fleet had been reduced to four vessels, only one of which remained under the British flag, and the collapse in that year of Irish Shipping Ltd. further compounded the firm's problems. Mounting debts and trading losses eventually forced the company to cease trading on 31 May, 1985, though vessels are still managed by a successor firm for foreign owners.

Sir William Reardon Smith, 1856-1935

Reardon Smith's first vessel, the City of Cardiff *was wrecked off Land's End in March 1912*

The Norwich City, *seen here after a collision with a bridge at Vancouver in April 1928*

The cadet-training schooner Margherita

The East Lynn *of 1928 was one of the firm's first motor vessels*

The Fresno City *was a wartime standard motor vessel built in 1945*

The board of the Reardon Smith Line in 1961, shortly after Alan Reardon Smith became chairman

The firm's first bulk carrier with engines aft was the Australian City *of 1964*

The Tacoma City *of 1972 at Cardiff in October 1984; this was the last visit made by a Reardon Smith vessel to Cardiff*

Hansen Shipping Company Ltd. — Norwegians in Cardiff

During and immediately after the First World War, there were many optimists in Cardiff's dockland, but undoubtedly one of the greatest was Sir Sven Wohlford Hansen, Bart. who was investing when others were retrenching. Like many other Cardiff docksmen, Hansen was honoured by the Lloyd George government for his services to the war effort and not only was he a substantial shipowner but he was also the owner of the lucrative Graham's Navigation Colliery at Tredegar. In 1919 he purchased the extensive Clearhouses Shipbuilding yard at Northam, near Bideford in North Devon and was the director of a number of ship repairing and ship chandlery companies both in Cardiff and Liverpool. Living in great style in Marine Parade, Penarth, Sven Hansen was obviously an important figure in South Wales's social circle.

Although Sven Hansen himself was born in Cardiff in 1876, his father Carl Hansen was a native of Bergen whose first contact with South Wales was in supplying pit props for the coal industry. He came to Cardiff in the 1860s and established himself as an 'importer of props and mining timber'. Very soon he became an important coal exporter and surveyor for the 'Bergen Ship Insurance Company and sub-agent for several steamship insurance companies in Norway'. He was also a rabid teetotaller who wrote pamphlets on the subject and was anxious to introduce Scandinavian systems of liquor control into South Wales. Carl Hansen's son, Sven, worked for 14 years at the Coal Exchange offices of the French company Messrs. Lucien Worms who were concerned with the world-wide export of Welsh coal. In 1910 he and his brother joined their ageing father in his shipbroking and importing company and for two years the two traded as Hansen Bros. Ltd. The partnership was dissolved in 1912 but Sven Hansen, in association with some other docksmen, created a very substantial business empire as shipbrokers, coal exporters and timber importers.

It was only natural that Hansen should have entered shipowning and in 1915 he purchased his first vessel — the 1891 built *Gledhow* of 2,661 tons followed in 1916 by another three vessels — the *Natuna, Ellerslie* and *Penylan*. In 1917 Hansen really entered the big time by purchasing the whole of Edward Nicholl's Hall Line fleet together with four vessels operated by the long-established Cardiff based company Pyman, Watson & Co. In 1918, despite many wartime losses Hansen was the owner of 12 large steamers. Not content with this he purchased a colliery and a Bideford shipbuilding and ship repair yard. Hansen was obviously one of the big spenders of Cardiff dockland, but during the slump of the early 1920s he was no more prepared for depression than his neighbours. Despite building three new coastal steamers between 1921 and 1923, he was in deep financial trouble; the Bideford shipyard was idle and most of his fleet was laid up. Five vessels were sold at the knock-down price of £76,000, two for £18,000 and the three coastal steamers were sold to Messrs. Stone and Rolfe of Llanelli. The business empire created by the son of a Norwegian immigrant crashed spectacularly and with its eclipse so too did Sir Sven Hansen, Bart. disappear from the Cardiff scene.

Sir Sven Hansen

Graham's Navigation Colliery, Tredegar, which was owned by Sven Hansen

The Tredegar Hall *was one of the former Nicholl steamers purchased by Hansen in 1917. (World Ship Photo Library)*

Frederick Jones and the Abbey Line

Frederick Jones was born in Adamsdown, Cardiff in 1868, to a family of Cardiganshire origins. As a boy, he was apprenticed to the well-known dockland iron founders, Tubal Cain, and through his membership of the Charles Street Congregational Church became acquainted with John Marychurch, one of the pioneer steamship owners in Cardiff. Having completed his apprenticeship, the young Jones was offered a post as third engineer on one of Marychurch's vessels and in January 1888 he began his sea-going career aboard the *Dewsland.* Thereafter he spent 11 years at sea with various companies, gaining his chief engineer's certificate in 1891 before joining Capel & Co. of Cardiff as marine superintendent in 1899.

Early in 1907, Frederick Jones set up the Melrose Abbey Steamship Co. Ltd. to acquire and operate the 1,211 gross ton tramp steamer of that name built in 1877, and two years later, he launched a second vessel, the *Tintern Abbey,* newly built by Richardson, Duck & Co. of Stockton-on-Tees. From then on until 1960, Frederick Jones was the managing owner of a total of 18 medium-sized tramp steamers, all bearing the *Abbey* suffix. They were chiefly employed on the intermediate tramping trades to the Baltic and the Mediterranean, though the firm is also remembered for its break into the North Russian Kara Sea trade following the General Strike of 1926, thus providing employment for its vessels at a time of manifest shipping depression.

Following the Second World War, the firm was left with one vessel only, the *Tintern Abbey,* built in 1939. During the post-war years, this vessel rarely visited South Wales ports, trading chiefly to the Mediterranean and, during the summer months, to the Kara Sea. The fall in freight rates that followed the Suez crisis eventually led Frederick Jones to lay up his last vessel at Barry in November 1957 and she lay there for three years until she was sold to Italian owners, thereafter continuing to trade until 1971. Frederick Jones died aged 93 in 1961, though the firm that he founded continues in existence today as a Cardiff-based investment company, run by his elder son, also called Frederick Jones.

Frederick William Jones, founder of the Abbey Line

The first **Margam Abbey,** *photographed upon completion at Gray's Yard, West Hartlepool in May 1930*

A cartoon portraying Frederick Jones's break into the Kara Sea trade in 1930

The founder's eldest son, Frederick Jones, who still runs the Abbey Line as an investment company from offices in The Exchange

The last vessel built for the Abbey Line was the Tintern Abbey, *seen here on pre-delivery trials in 1939*

The Glanhowny Steamship Company Ltd.

Many of the companies whose histories are outlined in this booklet — companies such as those founded by W.J. Tatem, Edward Nicholl and William Reardon Smith — were, in their time, eminently successful concerns, operating modern, up-to-date vessels that were capable of providing shareholders with fine dividends on the capital that they invested in those firms. Not all Cardiff companies were as successful, nor as reputable, however; many shipping firms established in the rapidly expanding port at the turn of the century had high hopes of commercial success that were never realised, and their story is seldom told. One such company was the Glanhowny Steamship Co. set up by Henry Bartlett of Cardiff and Captain Thomas Owen of Aber-porth in December 1903, and the history of the firm provides an example of one of Cardiff's many less successful shipping ventures.

Bartlett and Owen's entry into shipowning centered around the former Radcliffe steamer *Bala*, re-named *Glanhowny* after Captain Owen's home in Aber-porth. Built in 1884, she was far from being a new vessel, but the partners were confident nevertheless that shares in their venture would prove to be, '. . . an undoubtedly remunerative investment'. Their entry into shipowning, however, coincided with a prolonged depression in freight rates that lasted from 1901 until 1912, a depression that hit the tramp-shipping sector with particular severity. Larger, well-established firms running modern vessels could hope to cope with such adverse circumstances reasonably well, but small new companies operating one or more aged steamers, such as that run by Henry Bartlett and Thomas Owen, soon found themselves in considerable financial difficulties. The initial sale of shares realised only a little over half the nominal capital of the company, while maintenance costs on an old vessel such as the *Glanhowny* soon proved to be quite high and the low freight rates prevailing at the time barely covered operating costs. The situation became so bad that Captain Owen wrote to Bartlett saying that the only solution to their position regarding the *Glanhowny* was, '. . . to tie her up and sell her'. A further blow to the company came in 1906 with the death of Captain Owen while in command of the *Glanhowny* during a voyage to the Black Sea.

Following Captain Owen's death, the financial circumstances of the Glanhowny Steamship Co. became increasingly serious. As a result of the depression, no dividends were declared and then, on 25 May, 1907, the *Glanhowny* was lost by collision while on passage from Carloforte to Antwerp. Bartlett's intention after the loss was to acquire another ex-Radcliffe vessel, the *Mary Thomas*, but at a shareholders' meeting held in July, a number of investors expressed their lack of confidence in his managerial abilities, and tried to get the firm wound up. Bartlett's problems were compounded when it was revealed that he had insured the ship for £13,125, although she cost the company only £8,900 at the time of her purchase in 1903. Nevertheless, Bartlett succeeded in 1908 in pushing through the purchase of the *Mary Thomas,* re-named *Barto,* and the steamer, built only three years after the *Glanhowny,* was soon trading to the Black Sea. Bartlett was soon to realise, however, that his problems were far from over; the years 1908-9 marked the depth of the depression and in the summer of 1909, while unable to repay the loans on the new vessel, the *Barto* was seized by the mortgagees and sold. The proceeds of the sale proved insufficient to pay off all the creditors and in a letter that he wrote to the Registrar of Joint Stock Companies in November 1909, Bartlett described himself as being, '. . . absolutely without funds . . . there is not one penny with which to do anything'. The situation was quite clearly hopeless; the problems of operating an old vessel, costly to run and maintain, during a period of manifest shipping depression had proved too great to surmount and the firm was eventually wound up in February 1911.

Radcliffe's Bala, *which was bought and re-named* Glanhowny *by Bartlett and Owen in 1903*

The "GLANHOWNY" STEAMSHIP COMPANY, LIMITED.

INCORPORATED UNDER THE COMPANIES' ACTS, 1862 TO 1900, WHEREBY THE LIABILITY OF SHAREHOLDERS IS LIMITED.

CAPITAL - - - £9,000.

DIVIDED INTO 900 SHARES OF £10 EACH.

THE SHARES ARE PAYABLE AS FOLLOWS:—

£2 10 0 PER SHARE ON APPLICATION.
£7 10 0 „   „   „   ALLOTMENT.

DIRECTORS AND MANAGERS.

MR. H. A. BARTLETT,
AND
MR. T. OWEN,

Of Messrs. BARTLETT AND OWEN, Shipowners and Brokers, Bute Docks, Cardiff.

BANKERS.

THE LONDON AND PROVINCIAL BANK, LIMITED, BUTE DOCKS BRANCH, CARDIFF.

SOLICITORS.

Messrs. MOXON & LEAN, CARDIFF.

REGISTERED OFFICE:

MERCHANTS' EXCHANGE, CARDIFF.

PROSPECTUS.

This Company has been formed for the purpose, among other things, of purchasing from Mr. Henry Alfred Bartlett and working the Steamship "Bala" recently acquired by him from the Bala Steamship Company Limited.

Detailed particulars of the S.S. "Bala" are annexed to and form part of this Prospectus. She is classed 100 A1 at Lloyds and has always been maintained in a high state of efficiency and repair.

The purchase price of the Steamer is £8,750, at which figure the cost works out at the exceedingly low price of only £3.7.0 per ton, and the investment should unquestionably prove a profitable one in spite of the prevailing depression in Shipping.

Mr. H. A. Bartlett has had considerable experience in the management and chartering of Steamers, having been with Messrs. W. J. Tillett & Co., Steamship Owners, Cardiff, for nearly eighteen years, and is fully qualified to perform and conversant with the duties and requirements of successful Steamship Management. Mr. T. Owen has been in command of Steamers for a large number of years, and will act as Master of the Steamer.

It is only at a time like the present when the price of ships are at their lowest that it is possible to buy upon such exceptionally advantageous terms as this Steamer has been purchased, and, with this fact in view, it is with the utmost confidence that the shares of the Company are recommended to intending investors as an undoubtedly remunerative investment.

The S.S. "Bala" is at present on a voyage to the Mediterranean and will be taken over by the Company on her return to this country in about two weeks time.

The minimum subscription on which the Directors and Managers will proceed to allotment is 350 shares, and as more than that number of shares have already been promised by the Managers and their friends, allotment is assured.

The prospectus of the Glanhowny Steamship Co. Ltd.

The Kestell Steamship Company Ltd.

The Kestell Brothers, William Joseph and Charles Henry were born and bred in Cardiff. Both died in their forties — William in 1917 and Charles in 1922 — and with their death the modest, though profitable, shipowning enterprise that they established, was liquidated. The company was in business for only eight years but in those years substantial dividends were paid to the hundreds of small investors who had purchased £50 shares in the company that was established in the profitable years of the First World War.

William Kestell was born in Cardiff in 1871 and he worked for some years for the Ynyshir Standard Steam Coal Co., ending up as their commercial manager. The owner of that colliery was Sir William Thomas who was destined to be one of the principal shareholders in Kestell's shipowning business when that was established. When the Ynyshir Company was taken over by the international United National Co. around 1905, Kestell decided to set up in business on his own, but in association with his younger brother Charles as shipping agent and shipbrokers in Cardiff docks. Charles, born in 1878, was a well-known Cardiff figure and was a highly skilled player for the Cardiff Rugby Club.

The shipping agency business was a great success and for ten years the brothers ran an ever-expanding business from their offices in the Merchants' Exchange, but in 1915 with the huge demand for ships in wartime, the brothers decided to enter shipowning. In January of that year they purchased the *Thirlwall* of 1906, a vessel of just over 3,000 gross tons from the Mawson Shipping Company of Cardiff. This vessel was re-named *Holmesbank* after William Kestell's home in Dinas Powys and it cost the business a total of £30,500. In August of that year they purchased the 13 year-old vessel, also of 3,000 gross tons, from a London shipowner for £50,000. The vessel, the *Dowgate,* re-named *Seabank,* was to last as part of the Greek Mercantile Marine until she was torpedoed in 1941.

Capital for the new venture in 1915 was easily raised among the docksmen of Cardiff and of the 640 £50 shares invested, the Kestell family owned 220; the remainder being largely in the hands of small investors.

The Kestell Steamship Company was a well managed and profitable venture for the company in April 1916 declared a dividend of 38 per cent and recorded the purchase price of the two ships at £80,500. In 1917 the profits still amounted to £19,000 compared with a profit of £44,493 for 1916, but unfortunately, the *Holmesbank* was torpedoed and sunk in the Mediterranean in May 1917 and to add to the company's trouble William Kestell died in June of that year. This left the company with its single vessel — the *Seabank*, run successfully by Charles Kestell until 1921. In that year with the collapse of the freight market the company was in trouble and a trading loss of £5,709 was made in the year 1921-2. In April 1922 the *Seabank* was sold and with the untimely death of Charles Kestell in September 1922, the company was liquidated and the assets of £120,000 distributed to its many shareholders.

The history of the Kestell Steamship Company was short, but for eight years a highly successful, if modest company, ensured that its many shareholders obtained a fair return on their investment.

W.J. Kestell commenced his career in the offices of the Ynyshir Standard Steam Coal Co.

The Dowgate, *which later became Kestell's* Seabank. *(E.N. Taylor)*

57

Samuel Instone & Co. Ltd.

Samuel Instone was born at Gravesend in 1879, and at the early age of 20, he moved to Cardiff to take up a post as a shipping manager for the French shipping company, Compagnie Maritime Boulonnaise. This post involved the fixing of the French company's vessels with coal cargoes from South Wales, and with the experience he gained in this position he entered into business at Cardiff with his brother, Theodore, in 1908. Initially acting as coal factors and shipbrokers, they bought their first vessel, the former Morel steamer *Collivaud*, in 1914, and acquired further vessels during the war years.

With his extensive knowledge of the French coal trade, and being a fluent French speaker, Instone was a prominent member of the wartime Board of Trade committee set up to regulate the coal trade to the Continent during the war. Far from being a man of mere words, however, he time-chartered as many as 40 Scandinavian-owned steamers during the early years of the war, which he placed entirely at the disposal of the government, and acquired a number of other neutral vessels from South America to transport supplies to France. With the cessation of hostilities, Instone was in a very powerful position with regard to the continental coal trade, owning collieries in Yorkshire and South Wales, a fleet of ten steamers and operating agencies all over Europe. Carried along on the post-war wave of optimism, Instone ordered two further new steamers in 1919, but in that same year, he also moved into a very different sphere of transport.

With the dislocation evident at many ports during the post-war years, many ships lay idle while bureaucratic formalities were dealt with. Instone cut a swath through red tape with the establishment of an airline service to France: its initial purpose was to facilitate the operation of his ships but with his younger brother Alfred, a keen pilot, the Instone Air line was set up with a regular passenger service from Croydon Airport to Paris. The early 1920s saw an extension of this service to other European destinations such as Brussels, Cologne and even as far as Prague and the Cardiff-based shipping firm was soon at the forefront of the earliest developments in British civil aviation.

Samuel Instone's aeronautical ventures did not, however, enable him to escape the effects of the slump. By 1924 only three steamers remained in his fleet, all of which were sold the following year. 1924 also saw the forced obliteration of the Instone Air Line with a government recommendation that a single monopoly airline should be established. Instone's airborne operations ceased on 1 April, 1924 and his enterprise merged into Imperial Airways, of which he became a director. He gradually relinquished his shipping and colliery interests in the 1920s and eventually died in 1937, a remarkable figure who had foreseen what has arguably been the greatest long-distance passenger transport revolution of modern times.

Samuel Instone

The *Inston, completed in 1920*

The airliner City of London *was the pride of the Instone Air Line. (Science Museum, London)*

The wicker chairs and netted luggage racks of the passenger cabin of the City of London

The Navigation Colliery, Bedwas, which formed part of Instone's commercial empire

The Hain Steamship Company Ltd.

The Hain Steamship Company was one of the foremost of Britain's once-numerous tramping companies and their distinctive black funnels emblazoned with a white 'H' were once a common sight in the Bristol Channel. The company's origins can be traced to an old-established family in the Cornish fishing village of St. Ives, where Edward Hain is recorded in the early nineteenth century as part owner of the 1816-built fishing lugger *Dasher.* By the 1860s, the family were owners and part-owners of a number of small wooden sailing vessels that were engaged in the Newfoundland codfish trade and the Mediterranean fruit trade. The true founder of the well-known steamship line was Edward Hain the fourth, born in 1851; unlike his forebears, he showed little interest in active seafaring and went instead as a young man to London where he acquired a thorough practical knowledge of banking and commerce. In 1878 he returned to St. Ives, convinced that the future of the family firm lay not with sail but with the ocean-going steam tramp that was gradually gaining acceptance at that time.

Following protracted pressure from Edward Hain, it was eventually decided to order a steamer from the yard of John Readhead & Sons at South Shields, and backed by a loan from the Cornish-based Bolithos Bank the *Trewidden* was eventually launched on 26 November, 1878. She was destined to be the first of 87 vessels built by Readhead's for Hain, one of the most significant associations between builders and owners in the history of the British merchant fleet. Hain's association with Cardiff started three years later when he entered into partnership with R.A. Foster, a Cardiff shipbroker, to form the company of Foster, Hain & Co. With an agency thus established at Cardiff, Hain was able to secure outward coal cargoes to the Mediterranean for his expanding fleet of steamers, which then returned with grain from the Black Sea. By 1886, Hain controlled 11 tramps all of which bore names with the '*Tre-*' prefix: all were registered at St. Ives, generally in the name of single-ship companies. The fleet had further doubled in number by 1901, and in that year it was decided to amalgamate all the single-ship companies into a single limited liability enterprise, the Hain Steamship Co. Ltd., with a capital of £500,000 in £10 shares.

The company entered the First World War with a fleet of 34 vessels, 16 of which were lost in the ensuing hostilities. A far greater blow to the firm, however, was the death of Edward Hain's only son (also named Edward) in the Dardanelles in 1917. Hain was totally devastated by the loss of his son and died

The Tredinnick *and* Treminnard *were amongst the last vessels built for Hain's by John Readhead & Sons, South Shields*

himself shortly afterwards, whereupon Lord Inchcape, chairman of P. & O., stepped in and bought the entire Hain enterprise for a figure in excess of £4 m. Thereafter the company's head office was moved to London, but the Hain fleet maintained its separate identity within P. & O., with many of its daily operations being controlled from the Cardiff office first established in 1881. The association with Cardiff was strengthened in 1923 with the formation of a subsidiary firm, the Roath Engineering Co., set up near Roath Dock, in Cardiff to deal specifically with repairs to the Hain vessels. It was, therefore, during the inter-war years that the Hain Steamship Co. was most closely associated with Cardiff, and it was the company's proud boast that throughout this era a black funnel bearing a white 'H' could always be seen in the Bristol Channel.

Hains lost 28 vessels during the Second World War and emerged from the hostilities with a fleet of a mere 12 vessels. During the post-war years, the association with Cardiff declined rapidly; with the dwindling coal trade from the port, Hain vessels no longer called regularly for cargoes and with the increasing numbers of motor vessels introduced to replace war losses, fewer vessels bunkered at Cardiff. This situation, in turn, cast doubts upon the viability of the Roath Engineering Co. and in 1957 it was sold by P. & O. to C.H. Bailey and Co. By 1972 the Hain-Nourse company, as it was then known, was swallowed completely by the massive P. & O. General Cargo Division and by 1975, the once familiar 'Tre-' name had completely disappeared from the world's oceans.

The Trevelyan *was one of the numerous motor vessels built in the 1940s to replace wartime losses*

The Treverbyn *entering Cardiff in the mid-1930s*

The Chellew Steam Navigation Co. Ltd.

Truro, the county town of Cornwall, stands at the head of navigation of the River Truro, a tributary of the great natural harbour of Falmouth. In the 1870s, one William Chellew, a native of Devoran near Truro, was the owner of a small schooner, the *Hetty* and in 1874, he was joined in the management of the vessel by his son Richard. Foreseeing the ultimate demise of the wooden merchant sailing vessel, father and son decided to move into steam and by 1888, they had established the Cornwall Steamship Co. owning the *City of Truro* and the *Duke of Cornwall*. During the following year, they established three further single-ship companies, one of which owned the *Pencalenick*; thereafter all the Chellew vessels bore Cornish placenames starting with the prefix, *'Pen-'*.

Though registered at Falmouth, the Chellew vessels, like most British-owned tramp steamers, were to be seen regularly at Cardiff loading coal for the Mediterranean and South America. The firm had an office at Cardiff where most of their ships' outward coal cargoes were arranged, and until 1903, this office was managed by W.E. Hinde who was later to become a shipowner himself. The Chellew fleet expanded steadily around the turn of the century, with new single-ship companies being established to acquire new vessels as they were completed. By 1912, 13 vessels were managed by Richard Chellew, with another, the *Penolver* under construction.

During the First World War, six vessels were either lost or captured through enemy action, including the two most modern units in the fleet. This left many of the single-ship companies without tonnage, and in 1918, it was decided to rationalise the organisation of the firm by forming a single joint stock limited company, the R.B. Chellew Steam Navigation Co., under the management of Richard Chellew. Two years later however, increasing infirmity forced Chellew to relinquish the management of the fleet, and he was bought out by a native of Tiverton, Frank Shearman, who was at that date the manager of the Mount Stuart Dry Docks in Cardiff. Thus the Truro-based shipping company moved to Cardiff, with offices at 47 Stuart Street, Butetown.

Richard Chellew died at Truro in 1929 aged 72; during his later years he had been confined to a wheelchair. Following his death, the company that he had founded was re-styled the Chellew Steam Navigation Co. and in 1930, the management of the firm passed to F.C. Perman of London following Shearman's resignation. The majority shareholding in the firm also passed to a London-based consortium, who had to contend with the difficult years of the

1930s when many Chellew vessels were laid up, and reductions in the overall capital of the firm proved necessary. Five Chellew vessels were lost in the Second World War, as were three of the eight vessels that the firm managed on behalf of the Ministry of War Transport for the duration of the hostilities.

In 1947 the firm acquired a 'Liberty' ship, formerly the *Samnebra*, built in 1943, she was by far the most modern of the four vessels owned by Chellew's in 1947 as the others all dated back to the early 1920s. Following yet another takeover by Cory Bros. in 1952, the three oldest steamers were all sold by 1954, leaving the Liberty ship (now renamed *Pentire*), as the sole remaining vessel under Chellew colours. Shortly afterwards, in September 1954, an offer by the Eskgarth Shipping Co. of London to purchase the entire share capital of Chellews was accepted and the company ceased to exist.

The Pencarrow *arriving in ballast at Cardiff in 1947*

Frank Shearman of Cardiff bought out the management of the Chellew fleet in 1920

The Penhale *at Cardiff in 1936*

The former Liberty ship, Pentire *was the last vessel to carry the Chellew colours*

The Town Line

George Frederick Harrison was a Cardiff man who set up a coal exporting business in Cardiff's dockland in 1906 and for nearly 20 years the family business he established flourished and then collapsed spectacularly. In 1911 George Harrison was joined by his two brothers Osborne Walker Harrison and Tom Spencer Harrison, together with their father George A. Harrison, a Lydney man who for some years worked as a miner in a number of South Wales pits. In due course, however, he had become a manager in the bunkering and house coal division of Cory Brothers in their Cardiff office. George Harrison expressed a willingness to join his sons as soon as they had made a profit of £1,000. The shipping company they established was known as the Duffryn Steamship Company and in 1911 they ran two vessels, both built in 1899 – the *Claverdon* (2,085 gross tons) and the *Ormley* (4,158 gross tons). To this modest fleet they added the coastal steamer, the 1903 built *Woodland* of 244 gross tons.

The First World War was a highly successful and profitable period for the Harrison family. In December 1914 the company was re-named 'Town Line' and was made into a limited liability company with a capital of £1 million. They purchased new vessels so that in 1916 they possessed five vessels *Avontown*, *Bellevue*, *Benshaw*, *Holmtown* and *Woodtown* (the old coastal steamer *Woodland*). In those profitable war years the Harrisons invested heavily, notably in ships but also in the coal extraction industry. They became the owners of profitable anthracite mines at Ystalyfera in the Swansea Valley and the Global Collieries at Merthyr and Aberdare. They had offices in Swansea, Newcastle-upon-Tyne, Glasgow, Paris, Antwerp, Oporto, Lisbon and Hamburg with agencies in many Italian and Spanish ports. All was well with the Town Line, optimism was in the air, new ships were purchased and the family saw their profits soaring to a spectacular £144,222 in 1920. Things could not go wrong and in 1920, the Town Line was regarded as among the most prosperous of all Cardiff shipowning companies.

> 'We cut our own coal
> We carry it in our own waggons
> We ship it in our own steamers: and
> We distribute it in the home and foreign markets by our own agents.'

The whole enterprise was such a great success that no one in the Cardiff of 1920 thought the end would come so soon. By 1922 the substantial profits of previous years had been turned into a loss of £161,222 on the year's trading.

Some of the ships that formed the 19 strong fleet were sold in an attempt to stem the tide of recession. Unfortunately, in a greatly depressed shipping market only £3-2s per deadweight ton could be obtained from the sale of ships, whereas only two or three years before they were purchased for £20 or more per deadweight ton. The Harrisons were in deep trouble at a time of recession, but at a meeting of shareholders at the Royal Hotel, Cardiff on April 5, 1924, the Chairman, G.A. Harrison, presented his much acclaimed rescue plan. Attempts were made to restructure the company by reducing the price of £1 shares to 2 shillings per share. Even at the eleventh hour, an appeal was made for increased investment for the company he maintained was 'very sound and should yield a permanent ten per cent in the near future . . . for we are thoroughly satisfied that the Town Line must and will come again.' Barclays Bank, as mortgagees were not quite so enthusiastic and the five remaining ships of the fleet – *Kirktown*, *Lynntown*, *Johnstown*, *Parktown* and *Fifetown* were arrested, for after all the company owed Barclays Bank as much as £258,622 on loan and current accounts in addition to its many other liabilities.

Thomas Spencer Harrison was the first member of the family to venture into shipowning in 1906

Thomas was later joined by his father, George A. Harrison, in 1911

'Our own coals in our own wagons, sent by our own steamers';
an advertisement from 1920

The Ennistown *was one of the smaller coasters operated by the Town Line.*
(E.N. Taylor)

The Johnstown *discharging sawn timber at Cardiff in the early 1920s.*
(E.N. Taylor)

Evan & David Owen – two brothers from Blaencelyn

Despite the heavy losses incurred by many Cardiff shipping companies throughout the difficult years of the First World War, it was, nevertheless, a period of high freight rates without precedent in the memories of most shipowners at that time. A number of new companies were established in Cardiff during the duration of the hostilities, two of which were founded in 1916 by the brothers Evan and David Owen who were natives of Blaencelyn near Llangrannog in Ceredigion. Evan, always known in his native district as *Evan y Foel,* was the first of the two to venture into shipowning when, in March 1916, in partnership with E.L. Williams of Penarth, he set up the somewhat unusually-named Anglo-Belgique Shipping Co. with a capital of £30,000 to acquire the tramp steamer *Kyleness* which was soon renamed *Cymric Prince.* Williams left the partnership later that year and Evan Owen was then joined by his sons Alwyn and Aneurin; by 1918 they were operating two steamers both named with the prefix *'Cymric-'.*

It was in 1916 that David Owen became a shipowner when he set up the Bont Shipping Co. to acquire and operate a former Runciman steamer, renamed *Bontnewydd.* She was torpedoed in October 1917, but in April 1918, David Owen set up the County Shipping Co. which during the following year acquired two further second-hand steamers, renamed *County of Cardigan* and *County of Carmarthen.* With the eminent Cardiff shipowner Sir William Seager as a major shareholder, the firm did very well during the great post-war boom of 1919-20, but with the collapse of freight rates that followed in the early 'twenties, financial difficulties ensued. The *County of Carmarthen* was lost in July 1922; later, in January 1924, the firm found itself unable to continue trading as a result of its liabilities and was wound up six months later.

The difficult years of the 'twenties and 'thirties were also to have a detrimental effect upon the Anglo-Belgique Shipping Co. By 1930, its two remaining vessels, the *Cymric Pride* and *Cymric Queen* were partly mortgaged to Barclays Bank in an effort to improve the firm's liquidity and with the poor freight rates prevailing at the time, it was something of a tribute to Evan Owen's commercial acumen that his firm was able to show small profits during the period. Nevertheless, these profits proved insufficient to keep the company going, for in 1933, Barclays foreclosed on their mortgages and the Anglo-Belgique Shipping Co. was liquidated on 26 September, 1933.

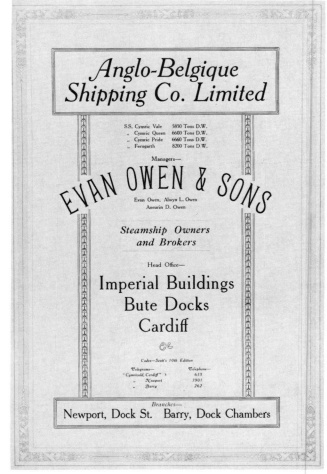

A 1921 advertisement for Evan Owen's Anglo-Belgique Shipping Co.

The Cymric Pride *was owned by the Anglo-Belgique Shipping Co. from 1918 until 1932. (World Ship Photo Library)*

Evan and David Owen were born and brought up not far from the coastal village of Llangrannog

The Deddington *later became David Owen's* County of Cardigan. *(World Ship Photo Library)*

The Emlyn Line

John Emlyn Emlyn-Jones was a very important figure in the business community of Cardiff docks in the 1930s and '40s. A local magistrate, public speaker, Chairman of the South Wales Shipowners and the Cardiff Pilotage Authority, he fought eight elections as a Liberal and served as Member of Parliament for two short periods. He was a broadcaster and an important figure in the National Eisteddfod. His father, Evan Jones, was a native of Llanwrda in the old Carmarthenshire and he came to Cardiff when he was 20 years of age. Like so many other people who came from rural Wales during the last quarter of the 19th century, Evan joined the Welsh Calvinistic Methodist Chapel at Pembroke Terrace in the centre of Cardiff and obtained work with another member who ran a flourishing coal delivery business. Evan, in due course inherited the so-called 'British Company' and he developed a very flourishing and extensive delivery business with a large stable of horses. His wife, Sarah, was from Maesteg and their home was at 1 Senghennydd Road. John Emlyn was born in 1889 and after being educated at Albany Road and Cardiff High Schools was sent to France, Italy and Spain for two years. He proved himself to be a very able linguist and on returning to Cardiff he joined the coal exporting company of Hopkin, Jones & Co. In due course he served as Liberal Member of Parliament for the North Dorset constituency.

In 1912 he set up a shipping company, the Emlyn Line, and purchased a small 370 ton steamer the *Queen's Channel* which had been built in Workington in 1894. This vessel, with its machinery aft, was renamed *Emlyn* and was concerned principally with taking coal, often from Penarth, to the ports of the Bay of Biscay and Northern Spain. Within a few months a slightly larger ship, the 544 ton, Montrose built *Eleanor* of 1894, was purchased and re-named the *Emlynverne*. With the addition of the ten year old, 450 ton *Emlyndene* in 1913, the company at the outbreak of the First World War possessed three vessels suitable for short voyages.

Operating through a series of smaller, one or two ship companies, such as the Bryn Steam Navigation Company and the Channel S.S. Company, the Emlyn Line possessed five vessels in 1917, most of them being small and specifically designed for the French, Spanish and Italian trades. In 1920, however, a new vessel of over 5,000 tons was purchased new from Irvine Shipbuilders of West Hartlepool and the vessel was registered in the name of the Dragon Steamship Company. This vessel named the *Emlynian* was to remain in the fleet until the mid 1930s and she ended her life as a Japanese ship sunk in the Straits of Malacca in 1944. With the 606 ton *Emlynmoor* of 1919 the two vessels were the only ones owned by the company after 1923.

Throughout its history the Emlyn Line was principally concerned with the Spanish and Italian trade, but with the takeover of Spain by General Franco, Emlyn-Jones became a severe critic of the regime and he was not allowed into Spain for many years. He objected publicly to Franco and he even established a home for Spanish refugees at Caerleon. As a result of the Spanish Civil War, the Emlyn Line ceased to exist as an active shipping line, although other enterprises such as a salvage company and the coal exporting and shipbroking business of Emlyn-Jones, Griffin and Company, continued until the early 1950s. The latter company managed 4 vessels in 1939. While Emlyn-Jones specialised in the Spanish trade, his partner William Treseder Treseder-Griffin was principally concerned with the Italian side of the business. In March 1952 the notable docksman John Emlyn Emlyn-Jones and his wife were killed in an Air France air crash at Nice and with his death the business was run down. His wife, Rhoda Penberthy Care, was also from a notable shipping family of Cornish origin. Her elder brother, Richard Penberthy Care, was the owner of the extensive Care Line of Cardiff while another brother, Edward, was of Care and Marquand, another flourishing shipowning company.

The Emlynmor *on the River Avon. (E.N. Taylor)*

J.E. Emlyn Jones

The Emlyndene dated from 1904. (E.N. Taylor)

The Emlyn at Bristol. (E.N. Taylor)

Edgar Edwards and the Western Counties Shipping Co. Ltd.

Of all the men who embarked upon careers as shipowners at Cardiff during the highly profitable years of the First World War and who later participated so avidly in the dizzy inflationary spiral of the immediate post-war boom, none rose so spectacularly or collapsed to rapidly as Edgar Edwards. A native of Ely, he was a shipping accountant at Cardiff during the pre-war years, but in July 1915, in association with Capt. W.A. Hepburn of Roath, he set up three single-ship companies, one of which was the Western Counties Shipping Co. that acquired the *Southina,* dating from 1899. This company realised a handsome profit during the war years, reflected in the regular increases in its capital, which rose from £10,000 initially to £174,000 by October 1918.

Edgar Edwards's finest hour came at the height of the post-war boom in December 1919, however, when the capital of the Western Counties Shipping Co. was increased to £1.5m. The reason behind this massive rise was to enable Edwards to purchase Sir Walter Runciman's Newcastle-based 'Moor Line' fleet, consisting of some 25 steamers, at a cost of £1.8m. The shrewd Newcastle owner had foreseen that the boom of 1919-20 was unlikely to last for long and that it would probably be followed by a dramatic fall in the price of tonnage; he therefore took advantage of the prevailing inflationary situation by selling his entire fleet at some £20 per deadweight ton. Edgar Edwards's optimism regarding his investment was, however, boundless; at the time of the purchase, he forecast that the massive fleet that he now controlled was capable of making a profit in excess of £1m. per annum, and he further increased the capital of the firm to £2.25m. in February 1920.

By the end of that year, the slump that Runciman and a number of other more far-sighted owners had foreseen descended upon the shipping industry, hitting the tramp-shipping sector with particular severity. Freight rates fell to a quarter or a fifth of those prevailing 12 months before and companies such as Western Counties soon found themselves unable to pay for the vessels that they had so recently acquired at grossly inflated prices. By April 1922 a group of Edgar Edwards's creditors had issued a compulsory winding-up order upon the company and the ships were later disposed of — many of them, ironically enough, being sold back to Sir Walter Runciman for about a sixth of the price paid for them only some two years previously.

Edgar Edwards

The *Lowmoor was one of the thirteen steamers purchased by Edwards from Walter Runciman's Moor Line in 1919. (World Ship Photo Library)*

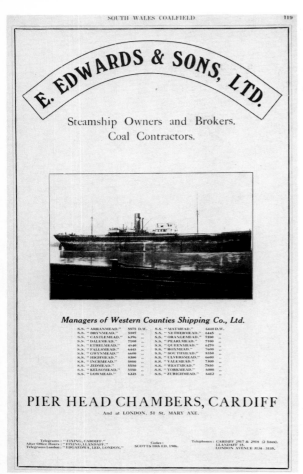

An advertisement for the Western Counties Shipping Co. dating from early in 1920

Goulds Steamships and Industrials Ltd.

James Childs Gould was the son of Richard Gould, a Penarth stonemason who originated in Devon. After a brief period at sea, J.C. Gould emigrated to the U.S.A. where he built up a New York based marine insurance company during the years prior to the First World War. Returning to Cardiff during the boom years of the war, he took over the management of the Dulcia Shipping Co. Ltd. in 1915. He sprang to real prominence during the immediate post war boom setting up in 1920 with his cousin, the shipping company of J.C. and W.T. Gould. Later this was renamed Goulds Steamships and Industrials Ltd., an amalgamation of the Dulcia Shipping Company; Griffiths Lewis Steam Navigation Company and the north-eastern shipbuilding and engineering firm of Richardson Duck and Blairs of Stockton-on-Tees. J.C. Gould moved from his home at Rectory Road, Canton to the impressive Dan-y-bryn (now the Cheshire Home) at Radyr and thence to an imposing home at St. Mellons. For a few years, all was well; the total capital of the new venture was £3 million and in 1922 it operated 12 steam vessels ranging from the 2,794 gross ton *Grelrosa* of 1905 to the 5,260 gross ton *Grelisle* of 1918. The *Grel* prefix for the names of the ships was an amalgam of J.C. Gould's daughters' names — Grace and Elfrida.

With the onset of the slump in the early 1920s, the massive undertaking established by J.C. Gould and his cousin only two years previously was soon beset by financial problems. A loss in excess of £39,000 in 1922 was compounded by protracted industrial disputes in the north-eastern shipyard. J.C. Gould who had been elected Unionist M.P. for Cardiff Central in 1918 was fiercely opposed to the retention of the wartime Excess Profits Duty which further hit the profitability of his enterprise. Eventually the difficulties at the Stockton-on-Tees shipyard dragged down the whole concern; on 5 May, 1925 a receiver was appointed and Gould's industrial and maritime empire ceased trading. For Gould himself it was a bitter blow; Dan-y-bryn was given to charity, the elegant house in Park Lane, London was sold and the mansion at St. Mellons was disposed of in an attempt to offset liabilities of £750,000 and more. But J.C. Gould's business acumen never deserted him. By the early 1930s he had set up the Mobile Food Supplies Company at Billingsgate, London which ran a fleet of fish and chip shops that were particularly well-known at race meetings on Epsom Downs. He was confident that he could embark on a second career as a trawler owner, but although his cousin remained in shipowning until 1960 as the owner of the old Jenkins Bros. company — the Cardigan Shipping Company, James was not so successful. He died in a council house at Coulsden in Surrey in 1944, a considerable come-down for one of the most remarkable of those entrepreneurs who participated in the boom-time of Cardiff's shipping industry. From ships to chips and a Surrey council house, James Childs Gould was certainly a remarkable character.

James C. Gould

J.C. Gould's cousin, Walter T. Gould remained in shipowning until 1960

The Grelhead, *showing Gould's distinctive white diamond funnel mark*

The Gould empire, as illustrated in an advertisement of 1921

A fine study of the Grelrosa *entering Cardiff, laden with a deck cargo of pit-wood*

Graig Shipping PLC

Of the dozens of shipping companies established at Cardiff during the boom of 1919-20, the Graig Shipping Co. is the only one that has survived to the present day. Set up in July 1919 by Idwal Williams, the son of a Cardiff coal trimmer, the firm acquired its first vessel, a standard First World War tramp steamer, the *War Down,* in October that year. Re-named *Graig,* her new owners were shrewd enough to realise that the boom would not last long and the vessel was immediately fixed on a two-year time charter carrying coal from Durban to Kenya at 28s.6d. per ton. As the freight market slumped late in 1920 (with other vessels being chartered at 4s.6d. per ton on similar voyages), the infant Graig Shipping Co. was protected from the crash by this fortunate agreement, and despite desperate attempts by the charterers to withdraw from the contract, the *Graig* completed her highly profitable charter before being sold early in 1922.

It was not until 1924 that the firm acquired its second *Graig,* followed two years later by the *Graigwen;* both were built new for the Graig Shipping Co. by Duncans of Port Glasgow and were employed chiefly on the River Plate trade. The fleet remained at this strength until the Second World War, but in 1940 it was augmented by the new *Graiglas.* The two older vessels were lost in the war as was the *Newton Pine,* bought in 1941, but in 1946 the firm rebuilt its fleet with three standard 'Empire'-type steamers that they had managed during the war, all of which were re-named with the *'Graig'* prefix. With the pronounced decline in the coal trade out of Cardiff after the Second World War, these vessels were increasingly employed in the world-wide tramping trades, and in 1951, Graig Shipping opened a London office in order to be in closer contact with developments on the City's important Baltic Exchange.

In 1952, the firm acquired its first motor vessel when it took over the Basra Shipping Co. Ltd. of London. Re-named the Glynafon Shipping Co. Ltd., it became a wholly-owned subsidiary of Graig Shipping. During the 1950s further motor vessels were added to the fleet and by 1959, the firm disposed of its last two steamships which had been laid up on the River Fal since January 1958. In 1964, the firm acquired its first modern bulk-carrier with engines aft, the *Graigwerdd,* built at Greenock. Three further vessels of this type were acquired during the 1960s and by 1971, Graig Shipping was operating three modern bulk-carriers. However, that year also saw the death of Idwal Williams, chairman and founder of the company; he was succeeded as chairman by his son, Desmond Williams, who had first joined the firm in 1945. Under his chairmanship, the company diversified its interests, acquiring a travel agency, property and interests in oil explorations in the Celtic Sea and later in southern England. A new company called Graig Exploration Ltd. was set up to manage the firm's drilling interests.

During the 1970s, the firm acquired a number of substantial bulk-carriers, but with difficulties developing in the world's bulk-carrier market at the end of the decade, a number of these vessels were sold in order to improve the firm's liquidity. By 1982, however, the Graig Shipping PLC was able to show a record profit in excess of £2m., and the firm has recently enjoyed a number of remarkably successful years despite adverse economic circumstances. Recent ventures have included the acquiring of interests in oil wells in Ohio and the building of a small coasting vessel capable of operating along the Seine and the Rhine, while the firm still operates bulk-carriers, of over 100,000 deadweight tons, thus ensuring a continuation of the long tradition of Cardiff-registered vessels in the world-wide tramping trades.

Desmond Williams, the present chairman of Graig Shipping PLC

The company's first vessel, the Graig, *was a standard First World War steamer built in 1919*

The Graigddu *at Cardiff in 1948*

The Graiglas *is typical of the large bulk carriers operated by Graig Shipping in recent years*

The Glynafon *on the St. Lawrence Seaway in the 1950s*

Charles M. Willie & Co. – the Celtic Ships

Charles M. Willie was for a short time a coal merchant and coal exporter in Cardiff and he established a business, that still exists, in 1913 when he was no more than 18 years of age. His father George Willie was a colliery manager with Cory Brothers and obviously the son was supplied with enough capital to establish his own business. Unfortunately, Charles Willie died as a result of a shooting accident in 1915 but the lucrative coal business that he had established only two years previously continued to flourish under the guidance of Willie's brother-in-law, Enoch Rhys James. It is probable that George Willie, although employed by a rival company in Cory Brothers was one of the main moving factors behind the development of the company, but obviously that connection was not publicised in any way.

It was not until 1929 that the first ship was purchased by the company. This was the 20 year-old 1,774 gross ton vessel the *Willodale* that was for many years, until she foundered in 1947, employed by C.M. Willie in taking coal from Cardiff to Bay of Biscay ports, especially Bordeaux and bringing back cargoes of pit props from France to South Wales. So important did this pit prop trade develop that the company opened an office to negotiate the purchase and transport of timber in Bordeaux itself. Although in the pre-war period the *Willodale* was the only vessel owned by the company, they did charter many others to transport timber not only from the Bay of Biscay ports but also from Spain and Portugal. With the sinking of the *Willodale* in the Gironde estuary in April 1947 with the tragic loss of 19 out of a total of 26 of the vessel's crew, C.M. Willie ceased to be shipowners and all the cargoes imported by the company were in chartered vessels.

The company, as the Draethen Shipping Company, owned the 960 ton steamer of 1946, the *Rudry,* which it ran from 1963 to 1966, but again most of the timber trade, now almost entirely with Portugal, was operated with up to a dozen chartered vessels, each about 700 gross tons in size. There was soon a demand for other cargoes rather than timber and by the early 1970s C.M. Willie was operating a liner service between Watchet in Somerset, in the main, and a variety of Portuguese ports. Other ports in the United Kingdom such as Mostyn, Shoreham, Newhaven, Sharpness and Goole were used and at present the company serves Spanish and Moroccan as well as Portuguese ports. By 1972 as many as 24 time chartered vessels were operated by the company and in 1973 their new vessel, the *Celtic Venturer* (2,500 gross tons) registered in Cardiff, and proudly carrying the red dragon of Wales, was purchased. In 1978 a second vessel, the *Celtic Endeavour* (2,500 tons), was added to the fleet. Today, from its offices in the Exchange Building, the company operates a fleet of four vessels and it charters many others for its lucrative liner service to the Iberian Peninsula.

Douglas Reid, the present managing director of C.M. Willie & Co.

The Empire Connell *was a German prize managed by Willie's during the Second World War*

The Willodale *leaving Bordeaux with a cargo of pit-props for Cardiff*

The Celtic Endeavour *sailing into Watchet on 5 June, 1985*

The newly-acquired Celtic Challenger *at Cardiff on 1 May, 1986*

Claymore Shipping Company Ltd.

John Charles Clay was one of the finest off-spin bowlers that ever appeared for the Glamorgan County Cricket Club. Living at Great House in the Vale of Glamorgan village of Bonvilston, he was concerned with operating the family shipping company that came into being in the optimistic days following the end of the First World War. That relatively modest company persisted until 1963 and as a symbol of the importance of its most distinguished directors, the funnels of its vessels in the 1950s were painted blue with two yellow stripes; the colours of the Glamorgan County Cricket Club.

The Claymore Shipping Company was established in 1919 by J.C. Clay's father, Charles Leigh Clay, the younger son of a distinguished landowning family residing in Chepstow. His father was a Derbyshire banker and brewery owner who migrated to South Wales in the 1850s in search of trade. C.L. Clay and Company, with offices in the Coal Exchange, was a highly successful coal exporting company with world-wide connections and it was only natural that in the prosperous years following the 1914-18 war that the company should have entered shipowning. In 1920, moving to new offices at Merthyr House, James Street, they purchased four vessels, two new — the *Daybeam* (3,023 gross tons) and *Daybreak* (3,602 gross tons) from north-eastern shipyards and two older vessels re-named *Clayton* (2,144 gross tons) and *Claymont* (2,406 gross tons) from other Cardiff shipowners. In the 1920s, although there were periods of idleness, Claymore's four vessels were principally concerned with the Mediterranean and River Plate trades. By 1928, the four vessels had been sold and two new ships were purchased, the *Daybreak* of 1925 and the *Dayrose* of 1928. Despite running two fairly new vessels, all was not well with the company in the late 1920s and early '30s and losses were incurred on trading every year with the result that in 1934 the *Daybreak* was sold to Greece, leaving the *Dayrose* as the sole vessel operated by the company. In 1936 the Fairwater Shipping Company and its one vessel, the *Fairwater,* was taken over and with the assistance of government subsidies the company's return showed a modest profit.

With wartime losses, the company possessed no vessels at all in 1945, but in 1947 it re-entered shipowning with the purchase of a 'Liberty' ship re-named *Daybeam* (7,233 gross tons) and the former *Empire Nerissa,* re-named *Daydawn* (7,036 gross tons), followed by another, the *Dayrose* (7,265 gross tons). All the company's vessels were sold in the 1950s, all for relatively large sums of money and in 1963 the modest company that was established in the halcyon days following the end of the First World War was wound up.

J.C. Clay

The former Liberty ship **Daybeam**, *seen in Cardiff's Queen Alexandra dock in 1950*

The Daydawn *entering Sydney under the harbour bridge in the early 1950s*

The South American Saint Line

The South American Saint Line had its origins in two tramp shipping companies founded within a week of each other in November 1926. On 17 November, Capt. George Buchanen Bailey set up the St. Quentin Shipping Co. Ltd. at Newport to operate the *St. Quentin,* named after the French town over which Capt. Bailey (whose father was the founder of C.H. Bailey Ltd., the ship-repair firm) had won the Distinguished Flying Cross in 1918. Shortly afterwards on 24 November, the Barry Shipping Co. Ltd. was established at Cardiff to operate three tramp steamers bought from the Times Shipping Co. of Cardiff. One of the directors and the general manager of the latter firm was Richard George Meredith Street (generally called Dick); a native of Penarth, he was only 25 years-old at the time, but was already an experienced ship manager, having started his career with J.C. Gould in 1916.

Due to his lack of managerial experience during what was a very difficult period for shipping, Capt. Bailey approached Dick Street in the early 1930s with a view to combining their fleets. This was achieved on 28 January, 1933 with the creation of the B. & S. Shipping Co. Ltd. that took over the management of both fleets consisting of a total of four steamers. Two years later, the partners took full advantage of the government's 'scrap and build' scheme with the ordering of three modern steamers from Thompsons of Sunderland. Delivered a year later, these vessels (all named with the '*St.*' prefix) were built with limited passenger accommodation and were seen by Dick Street as the nucleus of the liner service to South America that he wished to establish. Additional financial assistance to help Street realise his dream came late in 1936 with an offer of substantial backing from Lord Howard de Walden and Seaford; by 1939 the firm had established a sailing every ten days from Britain to South America and on 22 March that year, was re-named the South American Saint Line in order to identify it more clearly with its new-found liner status.

The company suffered heavily during the war years, losing a total of 12 vessels through enemy action, but with the cessation of hostilities, Dick Street was determined to revive the liner trade to South America. With this objective in mind, the firm ordered two new passenger/cargo liners of quite revolutionary design from Thompsons of Sunderland in 1945; the first, the *St. Essylt* was launched in 1947 followed by the *St. Thomas* in 1948. It was hoped that there would be sufficient trade to employ these vessels purely on a Cardiff-River Plate route, but this never materialised and by the 1950s, much of the firm's outward cargoes were loaded at Hamburg, Antwerp or London, using Dover as a passenger embarkation point. A third vessel of the same new design, the

St. John was added to the fleet in 1954, though the firm continued to employ some of its older vessels in the tramping trades. These trades proved particularly profitable at the time of the Suez crisis, and in 1960, they were able to order a fourth liner, the *St. Rosario.* Six months before she was delivered in June 1961, however, Dick Street died suddenly aged 60 years, and in view of the prevailing economic situation, Lord Howard de Walden and Seaford decided to wind up the company's operations. Due to various commitments in the liner trade, it was not until 1965 that the firm was finally wound up, when its goodwill and conference rights in the South American trade were transferred to the Houlder Line, London.

Richard George Meredith Street, co-founder of the South American Saint Line

The St. Quentin *was the first vessel of Captain Bailey's St. Quentin Steamship Co.*

The Withington *of the Barry Shipping Co., arriving at Cardiff with a cargo of pitwood in 1926*

The St. Essylt *is towed into Cardiff in 1948*

The St. Rosario *was built in 1937 under the terms of the government's 'Scrap and Build' scheme*

The St. Thomas *'dressed overall' on the occasion of her first visit to Cardiff in 1948*

Constants (South Wales) Ltd.

The Constant family were men of Kent and for 250 years or more they were concerned with maritime affairs on the River Thames. Some were watermen and lightermen on the river, some owned tug boats and dredgers while others were naval architects, shipowners and shipping financiers. Although the Constant family were substantial shipowners during the last quarter of the 19th century, operating a fleet of steamers from their London office at Billiter Street, it was not until 1929 that they set up a company in Cardiff with the name Constants (South Wales) Ltd. Undoubtedly the Constants — Joseph and his son, Martin, who owned seven or eight steamers — were regular users of South Wales ports in the heyday of the coal exporting trade. It is surprising that it was not until the late 1920s, when coal exports were already on the decline that the company should have formed its South Wales subsidiary. With the transfer of nine out of ten vessels to Cardiff in 1929 an office was opened in West Bute Street, although the head office still remained in the City of London. All the vessels owned by the company were named after Kentish villages for Martin Constant was a native of Gravesend, having been born in that Thames-side port in 1888.

The last chairman of the company, Roger B. Constant, when he left school in 1932, spent two years in Bremen, Bordeaux and Bilbao, ports with which Constants had considerable trade contacts. In the 1930s they were substantial shipowners and in 1936, for example, they owned as many as 16 steam vessels, all except two — *Lyminge* and *Offham* being less than 2,500 gross tons. Those smaller vessels were largely concerned with carrying coal from South Wales to the Bay of Biscay and Spanish ports together with regular voyges to the Mediterranean. The company had a contract from 1929 until 1939 to transport 15,000 to 25,000 tons of iron ore annually for Guest, Keen and Nettlefolds from Bilbao, Santander and Huelva to Cardiff, Port Talbot and Briton Ferry. Pit props from Bordeaux and Portugal, cork from Oporto and pyrites, phosphates, iron ore and esparto grass were also brought in considerable quantities not only to South Wales but also to Leith and Liverpool. The two larger vessels in the 1930s were more concerned with the River Plate trade.

R.B. Constant says 'When I started with the company in 1932, we owned eight ships — all purchased second-hand and I was told that the family's aim was to be able to build new purpose-designed ships for our usual trade. I can remember feeling that this would take a long time because in early 1935 we had six ships laid up . . . Towards the end of 1938 we placed our order for new building vessels. Two 4,700 ton vessels were ordered from William Gray of West Hartlepool and one 2,900 ton ship from Austins of Sunderland. Even in those days we would have liked to have specified oil burning machinery, but did not dare do so as we feared the loss of goodwill from our coal exporting charterers.'

At the end of the Second World War, Constants were left with three elderly ships that were sold immediately and three 'Empire' vessels were purchased. In 1951-2 William Gray of West Hartlepool supplied three new sisterships — the *Beltinge, Garlinge* and *Hawkinge,* specifically designed to carry a timber deck cargo and heavy goods such as iron ore. These three vessels were employed in world-wide tramping; taking anthracite to Canada, wood pulp and timber to Europe, sugar from the West Indies and sawn planks from Murmansk. The last ship purchased by the company was the *Lyminge* of 1967 and in that year the company still owned four vessels:— *Beltinge* (built 1951), *Garlinge* (built 1951), *Lottinge* (built 1956), and the *Susan Constant* (built 1958). The last was built for South Wales shipowners by Samuel White of Cowes, Isle of Wight and was regarded as one of the most beautiful vessels that traded from South Wales. By 1974 the business had declined considerably and only the two motor-vessels — the *Lottinge* and *Lyminge* — remained in the fleet. In July 1976, the business was finally closed.

The Lottinge, *built in 1918, was bought by Constants in 1934*

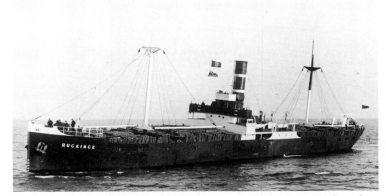

The Ruckinge *approaching Cardiff with a cargo of pitprops from the Bay of Biscay in 1936*

The Susan Constant *of 1958, discharging iron ore in the Roath Dock*

Lovering & Sons Ltd.

Though Cardiff was, throughout much of its history, predominantly a deep-sea tramping port, it nevertheless possessed a number of shipping firms concerned with coastal and 'short sea' trading. One such company was Lovering and Sons and the firm was probably unique among Cardiff-based shipping companies in that it never owned any steam-propelled vessels. The founder of the firm, John Lovering, was born the son of a master mariner at Bristol in 1887. The family later moved to Cardiff, and in 1906, John joined a firm of coal factors in the partnership of Barker, James and Lovering. This firm specialised in the export of coal to Ireland, and though based at Cardiff, most of the coal that the partnership handled came either from the collieries of the Forest of Dean (for which Lydney was the exporting port), or from the Point of Ayr Colliery near Prestatyn, whose fleet of steam coasters was often under charter to John Lovering and his partners.

It was not until 1936 that John Lovering entered into shipowning himself, with the purchase of a Dutch-built motor coaster bought from Bowles Sand & Gravel Co., Cardiff. Named *Calyx* by her new owners, she was one of the large number of economical and efficient motor vessels built in Holland during the inter-war years that provided a serious challenge to the traditional British steam coasters. Of light draught, carrying fuel oil in their double bottoms and cheaper to man as there was no need for firemen, vessels of this type were admirably suited to the trades in which John Lovering participated. So successful was the *Calyx* that in 1937 he ordered a second motor vessel from a Dutch shipyard, the *Teasel*, followed in 1938 by the *Cornel*. Carrying coal from Lydney and the Dee Estuary onwards to Ireland, they returned to Britain with general cargo from ports such as Belfast, Londonderry and Dublin.

The *Calyx* was sold in 1938, and following the outbreak of the war, Lovering & Sons were appointed to manage the Dutch-owned coaster *Tromp*. In 1941, they also acquired an Ardrossan-built coaster, the *Kindiesel* and the firm was fortunate enough to survive the war with no losses to the fleet until the *Tromp* was restored to her Dutch owners in 1945. With the death of John Lovering in 1946, management of the firm passed to his sons, Robert and Arthur, and during the post-war years the firm became increasingly involved in the general coastal and near-home trades as the Irish coal trade diminished.

In 1947, Lovering & Sons acquired the *Empire Punch* built at Lowestoft in 1942 and in the following year they also acquired the *Fennel* in place of the *Teasel* which was tragically lost with all hands off the Isle of Man in January 1948.

Further acquisitions were the *Staniel* in 1949 and the *Petertown* in 1951; these vessels were bought in place of the *Kindiesel* and *Fennel*, disposed of in the early 1950s. The fleet remained at a strength of four vessels until 1955, but in 1959, falling freight rates led to the disposal of the two remaining vessels, the *Staniel* being sold for scrap after a serious fire off Lowestoft that year, and the *Petertown* passing to Italian owners.

John Lovering, founder of the firm of Lovering & Sons

The Dutch-built coaster, Cornel, *sailing into Cardiff in 1949*

Arthur Lovering, one of Cardiff's few remaining coal factors, ran the company after his father's death in 1946

The Petertown *at Cardiff in 1956*

The Point of Ayr Colliery, Clwyd, whose steam coasters were often under charter to John Lovering. (British Coal)

An appeal

This booklet has dealt with the history of some forty of Cardiff's shipping companies, some well-known, others somewhat more obscure. Whatever their status, they were all part of the rich pattern of ship-owning that characterised Cardiff's golden era as a port of international significance. Throughout that period, however, there were probably something in excess of 150 shipping companies in existence in Cardiff at one time or another, companies about whom the present authors have been able to discover little or nothing. If any of our readers can assist us in some way with information regarding any Cardiff company not covered in this booklet, we would be delighted to hear from them. Write to the

Welsh Industrial and Maritime Museum,
Bute Street,
Cardiff,
CF1 6AN.

Tel: (0222) 481919

Index